STOP DRINKING ALCOHOL

Kevin O'Hara

Stop Drinking Alcohol

Copyright © 2014 by Kevin O'Hara

All rights reserved in all media. This book or any portion thereof may not be reproduced or used in any manner whatsoever without the express written permission of the author except for the use of brief quotations in a book review.

The moral right of Kevin O'Hara as the author of this work has been asserted by him in accordance with the Copyright, Designs, and Patents Act of 1988.

This book is not intended as a substitute for the medical advice of physicians. The reader should regularly consult a physician in matters relating to his/her health and particularly with respect to any symptoms that may require diagnosis or medical attention.

Stihlman Publishing Alicante

ISBN-13: 978-1502375445

ISBN-10: 1502375443

For Sean

Table of Contents

Introduction _____ 1

Chapter One _____ *9*
   My Drinking Past _____ 9
   My Alcohol Use _____ 13
   Time to Stop! _____ 20

Chapter Two _____ *28*
   Alcohol in Our Culture _____ 28
   Big Alcohol _____ 30
   The Alcohol is not to Blame _____ 34
   Alcohol's Healthy Benefits _____ 39
   Moderation _____ 46
   Brainwashed _____ 53

Chapter Three _____ *57*
   The Language of Addiction _____ 57
   Are You Alcoholic? _____ 61
   Your Recovery _____ 73
   The Symptoms and Side Effects Of Quitting Drinking 75
   The Demon Drink _____ 81
   Hitting Rock Bottom _____ 85

Chapter Four _____ *88*

- Fears 88
- Fear of Death 97
- Going to Your Doctor 105
- "Symptoms" after Quitting and Making Comparisons 110
- The Symptoms and Side Effects of My Drinking! .. 116
- My Quit 120
- Finding Perspective 124
- A Year and a Half through My Journey 129
- The Drinking Disease 135

Chapter Five *138*
- Recovery 138
- Cyclical Recovery 140
- Constant Damage Limitation 143
- Breakout Recovery 146
- Fuelling Your Body's Capacity to Heal 148
- The Body in Balance 152
- Your Body Immigration Officers 155
- The Psychological Aspects of Quitting Drinking .. 158
- Changing Automaticity! 169
- Moving Homes 173

Chapter 6 .... *176*
- Mindsets 176

Changing How You React to "Discomforts," i.e. Symptoms/Cravings/Side-Effects _____ 178

Habit Memories _____ 182

Benefits of Quitting _____ 186

Living Your Life like A Scientist _____ 190

Note from the Author _____ 193

Introduction

"Habit, my friend, is practice long pursued, that at last becomes man himself."
Evenus

Early praise for *Stop Drinking Alcohol*

"Down to earth and concise, stop drinking alcohol is a great tool for shifting the ingrained cultural perceptions surrounding alcohol."
Steamface - Amazon.co.uk

"Bought on first day and heartily recommend it. An excellent read!"
Albert Cragg - Facebook

"Great little book, Kev"
Ron - Alcohol Mastery

Praise for AlcoholMastery.com

"108 days clean now due to finding this savior/man at the right time.

*It's like screwing a wooden leg on every day, it has to be done every day in order to walk. This is a tough discipline too, it's gotten easier, but it's constantly around us in the modern world in which we live to entice us back down the slope again.
I thank you Mr. O'Hara for the no nonsense way you have handled your magnificent achievement..
Thank you Sir"*
Mark in London - on Alcohol Mastery

"Kevin – I love your no nonsense approach! I listen to your podcasts while I'm walking my dog in the morning and they inspire me to make positive changes in my life. Well done for maintaining great change in your own life while inspiring others. Keep it up!"
Holly - on Alcohol Mastery

"Thanks so much for this Kev – your videos are always helpful but this one really hit home – I'm on day 3 after a few false starts – your honesty sharing about your visualisation about your son really touched me, and has helped me to apply to my own situation concerning my own son, and strengthen my resolve going forward :) Thank you"
Mand - on Alcohol Mastery

Journey's Beginning

Welcome to *Stop Drinking Alcohol*. This book has come about after I quit drinking alcohol for good after many years of increasingly heavy use. I never imagined I would ever stop drinking… but I'm loving every minute of it.

I first decided to set up a YouTube channel and website just after I'd quit in 2013. My original intention was just to document my journey, to see what I could learn about myself and the process of change, and to use the videos as motivation to keep going. Alcoholmastery.com has since grown into a place that's helping people who're facing the same difficulties and fears that I faced; helping them to learn that stopping drinking alcohol is not as difficult as it's perceived to be, and helping them to find their own courage and commitment to abandon alcohol from their lives.

Quitting alcohol is liberating and there's every reason to start your journey feeling very happy about your decision.

Feeling Happy

Why should you feel happy about giving something up? For a start, because you are not really giving anything up, you're eliminating a poison from your life. This drug is a toxin that affects your body, your mind, your relationships, your work life, your home life, and your sex life. It poisons your perceptions about yourself and about the world around you. Above all, your alcohol use poisons the perceptions of the next generation and perpetuates the dangerous notion that drinking is 'normal', that it's not drug use, and that there is anything responsible about taking a poison into your body in the name of fun.

The moment you stop drinking is the moment you get to make a fresh start, when you get to look at your life through the beginners mind.

5% Alcohol

Stop Drinking Alcohol will show you that **your addiction to alcohol is mostly an illusion**. Like your average pint of beer, quitting drinking is only 5% about the alcohol. Everything else is getting a handle on your perceptions and your thinking.

You don't need to hide from alcohol for the rest of your life. This book will show you the true nature of alcohol within our culture; you'll see alcohol for what it is - a dangerous drug with no part to play in a healthy or natural life.

Life Long Disinformation

You'll learn about the propaganda and, let's be honest, the pure bullshit that make up the basis for our life-long beliefs that consuming alcohol is 'normal'. These fundamental beliefs are started from day one and are practiced and preached by the closest people in our lives.

We'll look at how the everyday language that we use can affect how we see things. We'll examine the use of words like alcoholic, moderation, recovery, and the demon drink. We'll also take a close look at how you can alter your expectations about the symptoms and side effects from quitting drinking by changing your thinking.

You'll learn about how your fears can hurt you before you even start on your journey and how making some small changes in the way you think will allow you to step across your starting line full of confidence about the road ahead.

Finally, we'll take a look at what you should realistically expect once you do quit. Most of us don't have to spend the price of a small house to get treatment; most of us can do it on our own. If you don't believe me, I implore you to see your doctor, get yourself checked out, and discuss with her* your plans to quit on your own. You'll find that she will be sympathetic to your cause, and she will be only too happy to provide you with any reassurances that you need.

You're Not Alone

There are millions of people who have already stopped drinking alcohol on their own without the need for medical intervention. They didn't need to be admitted to hospital, they went through no serious side effects or symptoms, and they stopped taking this drug without feeling any intense cravings to ever drink alcohol again.

From my experience, and from the experiences of millions of others who have stopped drinking permanently, quitting alcohol is mostly in the mind. If you can control your thoughts, you control your actions.

I'll be using both he and she, instead of the clunky he/she, throughout the book to refer to both sexes.

Speak To Your Doctor

Before we get into the book, I'd advice anyone who is about to embark on this wonderful journey to visit their doctor first. Have a chat with them and let them know what your plans are. They'll be only too happy to hear your great news.

The Commitment to Quit

"Commitment is an act, not a word."
Jean-Paul Sartre

The one thing that will guarantee your success is if you have the commitment to quit. If you are committed to never drinking alcohol again, how can you fail? You can't!

Quitting drinking alcohol is simple; you simply refuse to allow any alcohol to pass your lips.

Every alcohol habit is built on one mouthful of booze at a time. If you put a stop to the mouthfuls, you kill the habit. Job done!

Everything else is simply about adjusting and learning new ways of living your life.

Cross the starting line with the mantra - *I'm done with alcohol, no more*!

And that's it.

Start now. Don't deviate.

Start now. Don't deviate.

Start now. Don't deviate.

Chapter One

My Drinking Past

The First Time I Ever Drank

"In youth we learn; in age we understand."
Marie von Ebner-Eschenbach

It's a long time since I took my first drink of alcohol. I was 13 or 14 and, from what I can remember, the main reason I started to drink was that I desperately wanted to grow up. I didn't feel like a boy, I felt a man; but the problem was - nobody else did.

My best mate at the time was called Paul, but he was known as Molly because of his big head of rusty curly hair. During one of those long, hot, Irish summers (at least that's how I remember it!), we built a rickety shed in my back garden. We made it from old bits of wood, long strips of rusted corrugated sheeting, odd bricks, bits of plastic, and lots of cardboard. We christened it "The Secret Headquarters"; it was the place where we made our plans to conquer the world.

Try Beer - Get Drunk

One of our first plans was to try beer and hopefully to get drunk. The first thing we did was to get our parents to agree to us spending the night in the garden. Now all we had to do was buy the beer, wait until everyone was in bed, and begin our boozy experiment.

I can't remember where we got the money for the beer, probably stealing it from our parents. Our plan was simple. We'd wait outside the local pub until we saw a likely candidate that we could smooth talk and whose eyes we could easily pull the wool over. Ask nicely, hand over money, and hope for the best.

To our surprise and immense satisfaction, it worked first time.

We stopped this old guy who was just about to go into the pub. Looking back on it now, he must have known what we were up to before we even opened our mouths. Very politely, we asked if he wouldn't mind buying us a six pack of beer, saying that it was for our Mum who was sick at home and under doctor's orders to drink beer.

What type of beer, he asked. We didn't know any brands, so we told him it didn't matter!

He went into the bar and we didn't know if that was the last we'd ever see of him.

After an anxious wait he came out again, with a wink and a smile, and handed us a brown paper bag. It felt heavy. I remember hugging it against my chest as we ran all the way back to my house, laughing our heads off, full of excitement.

Ranking the Taste

I remember that first taste like it was yesterday. It was an Irish bitter called Smithwicks. I couldn't have chosen a more apt word for this muck if I'd named it myself: Bitter by name, bitter by nature.

It tasted absolutely rank. It's the one thing about that night that sticks most vividly in my mind.

I don't remember much after that first taste. I don't know if I got drunk on my 3 little bottles, if I threw up, if we were found out, or how soon we tried to repeat the experience.

I know this early drinking episode didn't turn me into a raving fan, that's for sure. I was still searching for ways to feel grown up and alcohol wasn't on the top of my list any more.

Unfortunately, the foul taste wasn't enough to put me off for life.

My Alcohol Use

"By three methods we may learn wisdom: First, by reflection, which is noblest; Second, by imitation, which is easiest; and third by experience, which is the bitterest."
Confucius

My alcohol use has followed a fairly predictable path over the years, a similar path that's been taken by many other drinkers. I bet you'll recognize some of this in your own life.

Like so many other users, even though my legal drinking career started bang on the day of my 18th birthday, the culture had taken care of the brainwashing a long time before I'd had my first sip. The day I was born was when the stage was set for my many years of drug use.

The Early Years

I was born in 1966, and that day was my first roundabout introduction to alcohol. It was the day when a few glasses were raised to wet my head, an Irish tradition. My mother and father might not have poured Guinness directly over my curly locks, although it's a distinct possibility, more my father and co took the time to celebrate my birth by heading to the pub.

Probably a few more bottles were cracked open when my mother brought me home from the hospital, and again when I was christened into the Catholic church - where more wine was drank, by the way. Even though I wasn't consciously aware of it, the seeds of my habit were being sown in my young brain.

Children learn most by imitation and who you become as a person is largely based on where and when you were born. If you're born into the western culture in the 20th and 21st centuries, alcohol is going to play a large part of your normal everyday life. On the other hand, if you were a male born into an 8th century Viking family, raiding, raping, and pillaging would've been a 'normal' part of your life.

Adult Drinking

Throughout my childhood, I always saw the adults around me drinking alcohol and never thought too much about it, that's just the way it was. My parents weren't alcoholics by any stretch of the imagination. My dad hardly ever went to the pub. He didn't use football as an excuse for a Saturday afternoon session, nor did he come home drunk looking for his Sunday dinner after an early house drinking session.

My mother drank even less. A glass of wine would make her giggle endlessly, like a schoolgirl, and she'd act silly for hours. She used to smoke in the same take it or leave it way. She'd make a pack of cigarettes last her for over a week. My mum's addiction was her kids, she had 13 altogether, with nine surviving the womb. She was one of the few real social drinkers that I ever knew. She didn't like drinking but she'd join in all the same, just to be involved, just to be sociable.

Like most homes when I was growing up, alcohol was used as a routine part of our family celebrations. There was more alcohol in our house at Christmas than at any other time during the year. My dad just wanted to have a bottle of every imaginable alcoholic drink, just to make sure he'd have something for everyone who might turn up on the doorstep.

A Normal Upbringing

Alcohol drinking was seen as normal. As a kid, you understand that it's only there for the grown-ups, but the closer you get to being grown up, the more you feel like drinking alcohol will signify your personal arrival to the adult world.

I grew up in England during the late 1960's and throughout the 70's. It was a bad time for work in the UK, and my dad finally decided to move back to Ireland in 1978, just before I turned 12.

As a side note - in the UK it's legal to drink alcohol at home, or in any private premises, once you're over the age of 5. Check out this page from the British Citizen's Advice Bureau.

18 At Last!

By the time I reached my 18th birthday, I could finally buy my own supplies of alcohol. Not that I hadn't been drinking copious amounts before I was 'legal', but by 18, I was well and truly hooked into the binge drinking culture. I couldn't wait to get into a pub to order my first "grown up" pint. I still hadn't "acquired" the taste for alcohol so I needed my Guinness served with blackcurrant flavoring and my lager with a dash of lime.

Now I could drink what I wanted, where I wanted, and when I wanted. I could get completely out of my face, stagger all over the place and puke in the streets, and that's exactly what I did, at every possible opportunity.

I was held back by the reality that I didn't have the money to live the champagne lifestyle. At first, I only drank on the weekends. Depending on who was buying and how cheaply we could buy our booze, the weekend could mean any time from Thursday to Sunday. It could mean a couple of pints after work, or an all-out binge drinking session that started on Friday, and lasted through to the early hours of the Monday morning. Many of those binging sessions would end only when I was so drunk and ill that I couldn't stand, never mind find my way home.

Alcohol - The Tool

Since those first bottles of beer in my back garden, I always used alcohol as a tool. It was something that was legal, easily available, and encouraged by almost everyone...

In the early days, I used alcohol as a way of blending in with the crowd, of being sociable, or to help me get the Dutch courage that I needed to overcome my shyness for chatting up the girls. I've also used alcohol as a relief from boredom, to escape pain, as a relaxant, and as a pick me up.

As I got older and began to feel the after effects of my binge drinking sessions, I started to use alcohol as "the hair of the dog," a way of hiding the symptoms of the inevitable hangover.

Behavior Modifier

This drug has been my default behavior modification tool whenever I've had any emotions I couldn't deal with. Instead of learning the skills and techniques to live my life and to deal with my problems, I've handled things by getting drunk. If I can't deal with a certain person, I'll get drunk. If I don't know how to manage myself in that situation, I'll have a couple of drinks and forget about the whole thing.

If in doubt, have a drink. If bored, have a drink. If tired, have a drink. If unsure, have a drink.

Eventually, drinking alcohol becomes the norm. Just as Pavlov's dog was trained to salivate at the sound of the bell, so we become trained to associate enjoyment or parties or fun or celebration with drinking lots of alcohol. Enjoyment and alcohol develop into constant companions, one becoming inseparable from the other.

Throughout my whole drinking life, I don't think I've ever spent a weekend without using alcohol. I stopped playing any sports as soon as I left school, unless I could play them while drinking. Alcohol was the reason I got very good at playing pool and throwing darts; they're both pub "sports", and I could play them while slowly getting pissed. I could also drink while I watched others play. The pubs and bars are always packed on match day.

Time to Stop!

"To study the abnormal is the best way of understanding the normal."
William James

Daily Dosing

I don't know exactly when it was that I started drinking every day. I got to the stage where I found it hard to relax without a few cans of beer or a bottle or two of wine. I started to need alcohol to do normal things like sleep. I never had problems sleeping when I was young, now I had to drink or I'd be tossing and turning for ages before I could drop off to sleep.

I'd often take a day off alcohol, maybe two if I could manage. I had to prove to myself that I could stay away from the booze. I wanted to displace any fears that I was turning into an alcoholic. My logic was always really simple, if you're an alcoholic, you can't go one day without a drink. If I could last a day without alcohol, even if it was only every so often, it was proof that I had it all under control and that I was handling my drinking.

Why Stop Now?

So what was it that finally made want to stop drinking?

There are so many different reasons why someone could finally decide that enough is enough. The decision doesn't come easy, usually it's after a lot of denying that there is even a problem. But eventually there comes a time when you start to weigh up your life. You look at your life and you clearly see that this is not what you expected; this wasn't where you thought you'd be.

The Catalysts

Maybe you've had a health scare. It could be a pain in the liver, a visit to the family doctor, or just the realization that you're not feeling that great any more.

Maybe your hangovers are lasting more than a day, maybe even stretching into two or three days. You may have reached the stage where the hangovers are becoming unbearable, where you need to have a drink during the day just to feel some relief, just to feel "normal."

You might be experiencing problems in your relationships. Your husband or wife might be telling you that they just can't stand it anymore. She has just handed you an ultimatum - either the alcohol goes or it's your relationship.

Or, like so many people, you've got into trouble with the law. In many cases, the catalyst is being stopped by the police while you're drunk behind the wheel of your car. You get a big fine, you lose your license, and you have to put up with the shame of standing in front of a packed court house while the judge issues his sentence!

Your Personal Tipping Point

In most cases there'll be one catalyzing event. This event won't necessarily be huge, or earth shattering, or even something that hasn't happened before. But it will have a massive personal impact on you.

Your personal tipping point might be just one in a long line of incidents and happenings, but it's the one event that finally opens your eyes to the life you are living and what you've got to look forward to if you don't stop.

DUI and Ten Months Off

That's the way it was for me when I stopped drinking in 2008. I was pulled over by the police in December 2007 after leaving a pub and jumping into my car for the short spin home. I was breathalyzed on the spot, arrested, handcuffed, taken to the police station, and charged with drinking and driving.

After the embarrassment of appearing in court, I was fined heavily and my license was suspended for a year. Things could have been much worse. I still think about how lucky I was to have been stopped that night. It was the wakeup call I needed to catalyze my brain into action.

There was no real damage done. I paid the fine, learned a very valuable lesson, and moved on with my life. Being stopped that night paved the way for my decision to quit alcohol permanently, five years later.

I stopped drinking before I appeared in court, and I didn't start again for ten months. Those ten months gave me the belief in myself that I could stop drinking long term. It took another five years, many other individual incidents and accidents, and one final catalyzing moment in late 2012, before I could finally motivate my pickled brain to take action.

New Life

How did I know it was time to finally stop using this drug for good?

My partner Esther and I moved to Spain in 2011. We had a lot of different reasons for wanting to make the move. For a start, there was the change in pace. I had been working in forestry for the last ten years and the damp Irish climate was beginning to take its toll on my joints. We also moved here for a change of scenery, and of course the year-round sun of Alicante played a huge part.

Near the top of the list of personal reasons, although I didn't broadcast this one too widely, was all the cheap booze. It's funny because I was even hiding that reason from myself. If you'd come up to me before we moved and asked me why we were making the move, I would not have mentioned booze. At least it would have been near the bottom. But as soon as we arrived here, it was one of the first things we bought - wine - and lots of it!

We made our plans, packed our stuff, and finally upped sticks and headed for the ferry in late November 2012. Despite lots of appealing from me, my son wanted to stay put in Ireland. Leaving him on the last day felt heart-breaking to me, but in retrospect, it was something that was good for both of us. He found some independence, thrown in at the deep end, and he kept pointing out to me that it was only a short flight to Spain and we could speak to each other all the time.

Fun in the Sun

Anyway, long story short, we moved to Spain and I saw Sean when he came over on holidays. It made no sense for me to make the journey back to Ireland, it was way cheaper for him to come here. Even though I spoke to him three or four times a week, I still missed him a lot, and I wanted to see him as much as possible.

Of course, once he was here, we wanted to have as much fun as we could. I'd save up some money and once he got here I'd take a week or two off work. As I've already said, fun to me always involved alcohol and Sean coming over on holidays was no exception.

I never stopped to think about the message I was sending to him, the example that I was setting. Of course it was always there in the back of my mind, but like anything else in my life, the solution to most problems, or any negative thoughts, was to get drunk.

The Final Straw!

By Christmas of 2012, I hadn't seen him for a few months, so I was really looking forward to seeing him and having a good time with all the family.

One night, a few days after he'd arrived, we went out on the town for a pub crawl. I can't remember exactly when we started drinking, but it was more than likely before we left home. Towards the end of the night, we arrived at a local Scottish "Celtic" bar.

We settled in and had a few rounds. Toward closing time, I ran out of money, and I knew Sean still had five euros in his pocket. I asked him would he lend it to me until we got home and he refused. We got into a stupid argument which didn't last that long, Sean eventually bought the last round, and we left the bar laughing. It meant nothing in the grand scheme of things and I really should have forgotten about it altogether. But the whole incident stuck in my head and wouldn't be shaken.

I couldn't get rid of the feeling of being a complete louse. I couldn't believe that I'd pulled a fight with my son just so I could have one more pint to add to the 15 or 20 I'd already drank.

Like I said, it was something and nothing. It didn't mean a thing. We're very close, but we often have words with each other which don't mean a thing and are always forgotten about. This time was different. Once he'd gone back to Ireland, the whole thing hit me hard. I felt like the entire two weeks had just been wasted. Instead of great memories of a great fortnight, I remember drinking, eating, hangovers, and that argument.

Finally, I saw how much I was wasting of my life.

It was my time to stop!

Chapter Two

Alcohol in Our Culture

"What fascinates me about addiction and obsessive behavior is that people would choose an altered state of consciousness that's toxic and ostensibly destroys most aspects of your normal life, because for a brief moment you feel okay."
Moby

Facts about Alcohol Use in Our Culture

Alcohol is part of our culture, whether we like it or not.

It's considered "normal" to use alcohol.

To stop using alcohol is considered "abnormal."

In terms of harm to the individual, and the society in which we all live, alcohol comes out as one of the most dangerous drugs available today.

Big Alcohol

"The highest possible stage in moral culture is when we recognize that we ought to control our thoughts."
Charles Darwin

The alcohol industry, or Big Alcohol (BA), aims to have alcohol accepted as a normal part of our society. BA actively opposes any attempts to control the overall use of alcohol or to recatergorize alcohol as a drug. BA is largely self-regulated, and although they say they have the best interests of the consumer in mind, those interests come after the financial interests of the shareholders have been well and truly met.

Pubs and bars are designed to make drinking alcohol as convenient and as comfortable as possible. They're also designed to make you forget about the outside world and to influence your mood and your behavior. Most bars have curtained or frosted windows so you can't even see the outside world going by.

Alcohol Propaganda

Alcohol advertising is everywhere. It's designed to make you want to drink more alcohol. Often, it's associated with bravado, with being sexy, with being social, or just being very clever.

One core message delivered by these clever propaganda campaigns is that alcohol drinking is harmless once you drink responsibly. Another is that alcohol use can be beneficial to your health.

The industry is at the forefront of promoting responsibility, but that responsibility is ultimately placed on you as the consumer, not Big Alcohol as the producer. In almost any other industry, if a consumer gets injured or dies because he has used a product, the company that has made the product becomes at least partly liable.

Not with BA.

Persistent Presence

Once you stop using this drug, the alcohol industry won't hold up the white flag, pack up, and leave you alone. Alcohol and alcohol propaganda are everywhere, you can't avoid it.

As you walk your dog in the morning, you'll still see the massive billboard that's enticing you to drink the best lager in the world.

As you sit down in the evening, watching your favorite soap opera, you'll still see ads for whiskey, vodka, gin, and wine, all trying to fill your head with images of beauty, fun, and the carefree drinking life.

For the foreseeable future, as you push your shopping cart through your local supermarket, you won't be able to avoid the alcohol on sale, or the tempting announcements shouted over the public address system, or the bottles of booze in everyone else's trolley.

You may well feel like you're the odd one out, the only one in the world who can't take advantage of this forbidden fruit. This is another clever tactic because we all want to fit in.

Scrape Off the Bullshit

The value we can get through understanding this bullshit can't be stressed enough. We've been brainwashed all our lives and the source of that brainwashing is not going to disappear. You can't stop it! What you can do, is adjust your thinking so that the bullshit has no effect on you.

Alcohol is a permanent fixture in our culture. If you don't change the way you think about it, you're doomed to failure before you even start.

You have to help yourself.

You have to take total responsibility for all your actions. You're already more educated about alcohol than most people. You understand that alcohol isn't the harmless drink that it's portrayed to be. You know the damage that using alcohol as a tool has caused in your life.

The Alcohol is not to Blame

"The best years of your life are the ones in which you decide your problems are your own. You do not blame them on your mother, the ecology, or the president. You realize that you control your own destiny."
Albert Ellis

The Alcohol Tool

It's true that once alcohol is inside your body, it can cause a lot of health issues. It can cause of a swollen liver, a saggy heart, and a pickled brain. The key element to understand here is that alcohol needs to be on the inside of your body before it can cause any of these things to happen. Alcohol can have no effect from the outside.

Blaming alcohol for your bad health, your bad behavior, or your bad life is just a cop out. Alcohol is a means to an end. We use it as a tool to shift ourselves from A to B. From being bored to not being bored, from being sad to being happy, or from being worried to not giving a flying fuck! There is always a reason to drink, always a strategy, even if that strategy is to get blind drunk so you don't have to think about your problems any more.

Our Reasons to Drink

There's always a reason to start drinking alcohol. Nobody starts drinking alcohol because they like the taste. If it were the taste that attracted us to drinking, our younger selves would have no problems drinking hard liquor. As it is, the more alcohol that's in a drink, the less we'll like the taste. Drinking pure alcohol, or ethanol, would not only be distasteful, it could also prove deadly. It doesn't take much pure alcohol to raise the blood alcohol content to dangerous levels.

It's the non-alcoholic components of the drink that we like, especially when we're young, when we're just starting out. We like the taste of the mixer or the unfermented fruit juice or the high fructose corn syrup, and so on.

We use alcohol because we were raised in a culture that uses alcohol. Growing up, most adults around us used alcohol. By the time we were old enough to drink legally, alcohol use was completely normalized in our minds.

Then we pass the habit down through the generations. I remember my father buying me my first pint and, passing on this wonderful tradition, I bought my son his first pint. I wanted it to be me who bought him his first drink. It's something that you do with your son who's just come of age!

Selective Drug Encouragement

Of course, as a culture, we don't think the same way about all drugs. Smoking, for instance, was different. I hated that my son smoked. I was so disappointed and fearful when I saw him for the first time with a cigarette stuck out of his mouth. I knew he was hooked straight away. It was just the way he held it in his mouth, the swagger that said - I'm a tough guy! I recognized it from myself, all those years ago when I was his age. And I knew that no matter what I said to the contrary, it would not make a blind bit of difference to him.

The point is that smoking is a killer, everyone knows that. And it's not something that someone with a right mind would encourage anyone else to do, least of all their own children. But I just didn't view drinking alcohol the same as using a drug. And like most of my peers, it didn't cross my mind that encouraging my son to drink was encouraging him to take drugs. If I thought he was taking LSD, for instance, I would have been mortified. If I thought he was mixing with people who were taking heroin, I'd do everything in my power to discourage him. But, in terms of overall harms, alcohol is far worse than heroin!

We send the message that heroin is a terrible and evil scourge on our society and that it must be stamped out at all costs. We impose massive punishments on anyone who's caught dealing in this or most other illegal substances. But encouraging our youth to use alcohol is fine!

The Nature of Booze

In terms of our personal use, alcohol is merely a means to an end. It's our drug of choice. If it wasn't alcohol, we'd be doing some other drug because it's not about the drug, it's about the result.

Alcohol is an inert liquid. It's not capable of doing anything on its own. It can't physically jump out of the bottle and into your mouth. It can't connect with your mind and force you to drink it. It can't persuade you with emotional arguments, it can't threaten you, nor can it plead its case.

You must be a willing participant. You deliberately have to raise the glass to your lips and pour it into your mouth. Once it's in your mouth, you must swallow each mouthful. In order for alcohol to become a problem in your life, you have to repeat this same simple process again, and again, and again.

It's worth repeating here that quitting alcohol is very, very simple. You simply refuse to partake. You don't buy it, you don't pour it, and you don't drink it.

If this is the only step you ever take, you will end your alcohol problems for good.

How can you have a problem with alcohol if you don't drink it?

Stopping drinking the stuff is the first simple step. Next, you can start to break apart the life that you've built around your drinking.

Alcohol's Healthy Benefits

"Advertising is legalized lying."
H. G. Wells

The Invisible Hand

As far back as I can remember, there's been a connection between health and consuming alcohol in moderation. Every so often, you'll read an article which extols the health benefits of drinking wine or beer or whatever alcoholic drink happens to be in vogue at the time.

Once you start delving into some of the stories, you'll find that most of them are myths at best, and downright lies at worst. Somewhere lurking in the background of most of these "health benefit" stories is the invisible hand of an alcohol manufacturer.

Healthy Binge Drinking?

Besides, even if all the alcohol benefit stories were true, they wouldn't make a blind bit of difference to you and me. Why? Because any alleged health benefits from drinking alcohol are always associated with moderate drinking, not daily binge drinking.

The reason we heavy drinkers convince ourselves that there are health benefits to drinking alcohol is because we don't really want to quit. We're way too cozy, sitting in our comfort zones, to really want to break out and change our behavior. We like what we're doing, even though we might not like some of the consequences.

When we hear that there are health benefits to drinking wine or beer, we conveniently don't hear, or choose not to hear, the part about drinking moderately. BA is well clued in to this human foible.

What is Safe Drinking?

Another issue is that nobody can agree on what counts as moderate drinking or what is considered to be safe. One group might say that one unit for women and two units for men, on any one occasion, is the safe way to drink. Another will tell you that you can have one drink if you're a woman and two drinks if you're a man. Then there are different rules for how many units or drinks you can consume in a week, or if it's safe to drink every day. It also depends on how old you are, how much you weigh, how tall you are, your present health, and so on.

Once a person starts drinking, do you really think she is going to take out a little pocket calculator and start doing the math about how much they have left to drink? It's even less likely when nobody is sure about the figures. BA knows this only too well.

Moot Point

If you're drinking way too much alcohol, and if you've tried to moderate your use and failed, what difference does it make to you if there are health benefits to drinking small amounts? You don't drink small amounts! If you did, you wouldn't be reading this book.

It's one of the lies I told myself over and over again. I was convinced that wine was great for my health. All my knowledge was based on no facts, just speculations that I had gathered over the years and twisted to fit my own logic. Red wine would thin my blood, which in turn would make it less likely that I would have a heart attack.

I never bothered to look into any of the claims for the simple reason that I didn't want to know. I didn't want to risk finding out any truths. What if I found information that sparked small doubts. No, no, no, I just couldn't risk it! It wasn't that I'd made the conscious decision not to look for truthful information; I just didn't feel the need. I already knew all I needed to know. It's just the way we humans are wired. And I can't remember where I learned these nuggets of great news about my good health. It could have been written on the back of a toilet door, it doesn't really matter.

Looking For the Sticky Tape

If you start digging around, you have to be prepared to not like what you find. The more you dig, the more chance you have of uncovering some piece of information that plants little seeds of doubt in your mind. We don't want these nasty little seeds spoiling our hooched-up fun. We don't want to spoil the party with the "truth", so we don't look. Ignorance is bliss!

Now that I've stopped drinking, I love having a dig around. When I see a study or a report about some crazy new benefit from drinking alcohol, I start looking for the strings, the tape, and the glue. And to be honest, they're never that hard to find.

The alcohol industry spends an awful lot of money in getting to know us really well. Many of the world's leading psychologists are netting huge salaries and bonuses while working for the alcohol industry. Their job is to figure out exactly what makes us tick. There is no guess work in alcohol marketing and propaganda. The bottles are shaped to push your buttons, as are the labels, and the bar pumps. The whole experience, from the billboard advertising and TV promotions and how the pubs are laid out, is designed to excite your emotions.

Behind most "scientific" studies, reports, and findings, some of them from very well respected authorities and scientists, you'll almost always find the hand and super large wallets of BA.

Protecting You from Yourself

At the end of the day, does any of this matter? Alcohol is a poison! It's the end product of rotting fruit, vegetables, or grains. Look at the violent reaction the human body has when alcohol is consumed for the first time. Vomiting is part of the body's defense system; it's the way your body reacts if you swallow any poison. It's only when you continually persist in drinking alcohol that your body starts to develop a tolerance. This, too, is part of the defensive system. Alcohol tolerance is not meant as a measure of how hard you are, or how much alcohol you can handle; it's your body trying to protect you from yourself.

We kid ourselves into believing that drinking alcohol is something that's very natural, that we've been doing it for thousands of years. If it's so natural, how come our bodies go through this brutal reaction when we first drink it?

The only natural alcohol intoxication comes from eating over-ripe fruit or through your body's normal digestive processes. The reason your body is capable of dealing with these small amounts of alcohol is because of how t has evolved over millions of years.

Because of the huge amounts of rotting fruit you'd need to consume to get a buzz, it's impossible to get addicted to the alcohol in this way. A second reason is because fruit is seasonal. It's only available for a couple of months of the year, and over-ripe fruit is around for a couple of days max.

Manufactured alcohol certainly isn't natural. There are no physical restrictions on how much you can consume or over what period. Drinking a lot of manufactured alcohol introduces alarming amounts of toxins into your body, which in turn causes your body to work very hard just to keep you alive. The more you drink, the harder your body has to work. But there are limits to how much your body can take.

Moderation

"Complete abstinence is easier than perfect moderation."
Saint Augustine

Lifelong Restraint

Is alcohol the only drug where moderation is even suggested? Is it the only drug that has the "responsible" label attached to its use?

If you told your doctor you were addicted to heroin, what would she say - Moderation's the way to go? Cut back on the amount you're injecting!

Moderation means restraint. It means holding yourself back, not letting yourself go to the level that you really want to go. Is that what you want? To be forever holding yourself back? Could you really live the rest of your life like that, forever denying yourself the whole reason for drinking?

Drinking to Drunk

Is drug moderation possible? Alcohol is a substance that reduces your competency. It also reduces your inhibitions. Once you start drinking, you'll find it hard to say no to a second round. Once you've had the second, you'll find it even more difficult to say no to the third. Once you've had the third ... well, you know where I'm going with this. That's the life of a person who likes to drink until drunk.

Have you ever tried to moderate your drinking?

How successful were you?

Crash Moderation!

If you're anything like me, alcohol moderation might look something like this.

You stop drinking during the week. Perhaps you decide you're only going to drink on Tuesdays, Thursdays, Fridays, and Saturdays. You won't touch a drop for the other three days. Or maybe you choose to only drink at the weekend: Friday, Saturday, and Sunday.

You manage to stick to your non-drinking days, although not without thinking about drinking while you're on your "days off". You say that the weekend will soon be here and that once Friday afternoon arrives you can let your hair down and enjoy yourself.

You wake up Friday morning. All day long you anticipate your first drink. You're almost salivating by the end of the day and you can't wait to get to the pub, to the restaurant, or home to get that first taste.

Once you start drinking you keep going. After all, this is the reason you've sacrificed all week long - your well-deserved reward. You don't set yourself limits on how much you can have on your "drinking" days, you just go for it. Not drinking all week was moderation enough. You congratulate yourself for a job well done. It's time for you to let your hair down and celebrate ... you did it! You restrained yourself all week long! Yay!

You may have also tried moderating the amounts of alcohol you consume in any one session. Maybe you go out with the intention of only having four drinks instead of your usual ten. You've even succeeded a couple of times, which only goes to prove that you have no problem with alcohol, that you can take it or leave it.

Moderating your drinking once you've started drinking is way harder than taking a full day off. When you take a day off, you just put it out of your mind as best you can and get on with your day. Once you've had a drink, however, the urge to continue always gets stronger. One drink gives rise to another; it's cause and effect.

Moderation only makes sense in a world of moderation. We don't live in that world. We live in a world where excess is king.

Forever Moderating

Moderation is open ended. It's something you must do for the rest of your life. You can't do it for a week and then move on. You have to moderate every day of the week, every week, every month, and every year. Are you up for that? Is that something you want? Do you have the self-control, the balance, or the patience to continue to moderate forever? Do you have the lifelong strength to moderate when all you really want to do is get drunk?

How is that easier than just removing alcohol from the equation? Stopping drinking is a task you only have to complete once. You stop and that's it! So long as you don't restart, you're done!

Using to Abusing

My alcohol-drinking life has always been drink to get drunk, use to abuse. I've tried moderation and I was fucking miserable for most of the time. I'd always last a couple of weeks, and then I'd simply go back to normal, no fuss. I'd just go right back to drinking whenever I felt like it.

When I tried moderation, I don't think I drank any less alcohol overall. I just drank less or none during the week and way more at the weekends, or whatever days I chose to drink. Why? Because I knew I'd be right back on the moderation diet tomorrow. I knew I wouldn't get the chance to "enjoy" myself for another few days, so I might as well go the whole hog right now.

Tolerance Compared

I know the nature of alcohol and the effect it's had on me. It's a drug. The longer you use it, the more your body fights against it by making you immune to the effects. The more immune you get to the effects, the more you need to get the same buzz.

There are some drugs, like LSD, where tolerance builds up very quickly. You can only take so much and that's it. It's useless to take any more because you won't get high.

That's not the case with alcohol. The more tolerant your body becomes, the more you need, period. The more you need, the more you use, the more you use, the more you need. All the while, the damage is accumulating.

Can I Moderate My Drinking?

When I was drinking alcohol, the desire to drink was insatiable. It was always there. Moderation was impossible for me because I didn't drink for moderation. Once I couldn't drink alcohol to get drunk, what was the point? Could I have learned to use alcohol in moderation? If I'm being honest, I think it would have driven me mad.

We live in a world of manipulation and exploitation. Vast sums of money are spent every day in researching and developing ways to control your mental wiring, looking for what makes you tick, and seeking out the methods to exploit those weaknesses for profit. The best possible customer is an addicted customer. When you're an addicted customer, you essentially become a slave to the product, whether that product happens to be alcohol, cigarettes, or your favorite brand of soft drink.

Do I think that I could moderate my drinking into the future? I probably could, yeah. Why would I want to put myself through that kind of hell? I don't see any personal gain in being smashed out of my head anymore and I've no desire to drink just for the taste, there are plenty of tastier things out there.

Brainwashed

"Emancipate yourselves from mental slavery. None but ourselves can free our minds."
Bob Marley

Preaching to the Choir

Moderation is a great brainwashing tactic. It's keeps us drinking. The alcohol does the rest. By playing the moderation card, we continue to see alcohol as a benign substance, especially when it's classified as a beverage, not a drug. Once you've taken your first drink, the alcohol can do its job. Alcohol makes you a little thirsty, you get a little more relaxed and a little less likely to say no, it's so easy to say - *I'll just have the one more.*

Heavy drinkers or alcoholics, whatever you want to call them, are the bread and butter of the alcohol industry. BA doesn't need to waste propaganda time or dollars on the heavy drinker. We're all self-propagandized enough. The only choice we make is what brand to drink. And even there, where's the choice! I was a Guinness man. No other brand would do. Not Beamish, nor Murphy's, not even O'Hara's.

Marketing the Youth

BA, like Big Tobacco, concentrates most of their marketing money on building for the future. They aim all their ammunition towards the young. And the industry freely admits this. You'll rarely see any of their propaganda messages aimed at old farts sitting on bar stools in the local pub. Every advert depicts youth, strength, vitality, daring, sex, good looks, and so on. Then these depictions are associated with the alcoholic product. It's all basic Pavlovian conditioning.

Young Lads on the Piss

Let's take an example of a typical group of lads having a night on the town. At the most extreme level of the moderation scale, you're allowed 14 alcoholic drinks in a week, with no one day exceeding 4 drinks.

Among our group of lads, there's one guy who's on the local soccer team and he's trying to keep his drinking in check, he doesn't want to go above the four drinks on one night rule. It doesn't take very long before he reaches his limit and decides enough is enough. He has a choice, he leaves the bar and goes home or he sticks around but only has soft drinks for the rest of the night.

Because he's already had his limit of four pints at this stage, his aggression levels might be slightly raised and his inhibitions will definitely be lowered. Everyone else is continuing to knock back the pints and they're more than likely taking the piss out of our moderation lad.

He ignores all the remarks and soldiers on. By the end of the night he's all sobered up, but his mates are completely drunk, shouting and balling, and just carrying on in general. They're on two completely different levels. He's now wishing he hadn't stuck around after all.

How many times will he put up with that situation? Most lads won't even get to the first soft drink. As soon as the piss taking starts, they'll either carry on drinking alcohol or they'll leave.

Early Influencer's

The brainwashing starts early and carries on throughout your life. It comes at you from all angles. Your first brainwasher's are probably your parents and their friends, the TV, the posters that you see on your way to school, maybe even your teachers. If you went to church as a kid, you might have seen alcohol as part of the service.

Alcohol is used at every celebration, parties, birthdays, Christmas, Easter, graduations, christenings, weddings, and funerals.

You are also a big part of your own brainwashing, especially once you start drinking.

You develop certain alcohol rituals over the years. You get used to things being done in a certain way - you like to drink from a particular type of glass, you'll get used to a favorite beer, a way of drinking that beer, and most of your friends will tend to drink similar types of alcohol.

Chapter Three

The Language of Addiction

"Victorious warriors win first and then go to war, while defeated warriors go to war first and then seek to win"
Sun Tzu, The Art of War

Extracting Meaning

Our language is like a massive box of tools. Each word within that language is a separate tool. Imagine the sorts of tools you would find in a toolbox, a hammer, a chisel, a saw, a file, a bottle of glue, a paint brush, or a nail. Each of these tools has a different function. The same thing goes for each word or sentence in your language toolbox. We use our language to understand what's going on in the "outside" world and to communicate what's happening in our "inside" world.

Most words in our language have several different meanings. For instance, according to the website, dictionary.com, there are 26 meanings for the word *dog*.

Your idea of a dog might be completely different to mine, but in general we can agree that a dog is a four legged animal that barks and wags its tail. It could be a big dog like a Great Dane, or a small dog like a Pekingese. They're both dogs, in the general sense of the word, but really quite different. There are hairy dogs and bald dogs. There are dogs that have deep base barks and others that have high squeaky, persistent and very annoying barks.

The same sort of logic applies to any solid thing. If you can physically touch something, you should be able to describe it so that the other person gets what you're on about. If I say the word chair, you understand immediately that what I am talking about is something you sit on or stand on to change a light bulb. The same applies to every noun like door, apple, gate, computer, pen, weasel, and so forth.

If I'm trying to describe an apple to you and you don't speak any English, I'm going to have some difficulty. I could say the word apple, over and over, all day long and you wouldn't understand what the hell I'm on about. I could try to mime out the shape of an apple, mimic an apple falling from a tree, or I could pretend I was eating an apple, and so on. But if I pull an apple from my pocket and hold it up in front of your face, you'll get it straight away. Even if you've never seen an apple before, you'll understand that's it's a type of fruit.

Tools or Weapons

You can't use the same process for describing words like love, hate, jealousy, or emotion. These are words that have no physical object. I can't just pull some hate or love out of my pocket and hold it up for you to examine. Even though I can write the words love and hate, maybe on my knuckles, the words are only representations for something that has no material basis. There is nothing that you can point to and say *that's love* or *here is some hate*. These words mean something different to everyone.

Let's take a closer look at the word *love*. You can't point to love and it is often very difficult to describe. One of the ways we can try to communicate *love* is in terms of feelings; *I feel butterflies in my stomach when I think of you* or *my heart flutters when you're near*. We can also try to represent love by using solid objects like a heart, red roses, or even a well-worn but treasured photograph. We can attempt to define love by talking about other abstractions such as happiness, caring, passion, or forever.

So, when you try to communicate your understanding of the word love, there are certain aspects of your depiction that we will all be able to understand; then there are certain aspects that only some of us will understand, and there are aspects that nobody else will understand except you. This is the same with all abstracts. Beauty is in the eye of the beholder. So is anger. So is jealousy. So is problem, solution, good, bad, or deviant.

So is alcoholic!

Are You Alcoholic?

"Words are, of course, the most powerful drug used by mankind."
Rudyard Kipling

The Perception of Alcoholic

Alcoholic is a word which has many meanings, depending on who's using it. A doctor will use it to define a condition or a disease. A judge might use it to ascertain culpability in a crime. A job interviewer might see it as trouble in the making. A member of AA might see it as a permanent illness.

It's a word that nobody wants to be attached to themselves. It's a word that has prevented many heavy drinkers from even admitting to themselves that they might have a small alcohol problem. In perception, there's a fine line between problem drinker and alcoholic!

What are the common perceptions of alcoholic and alcoholism? Alcoholism is commonly perceived as bad. To be an alcoholic is a label that can stick with you for the rest of your life. Once you're known as an alcoholic, you'll be perceived as weak, troubled, pathetic, or out of control, a lesser person who's incapable of handling their drink.

The alcohol industry reinforces this perception by promoting 'responsibility' and 'safe' levels of consumption. At the same time, Big Alcohol spends hundreds of billions of dollars connecting alcohol to the good life, to strength and virility, to sexiness and passion. The goal of BA is to increase consumption and profits, maintain and grow brand loyalty, while at the same time distancing itself and its products from any problems that come about from its use.

Should You Call Yourself an Alcoholic?

How does this all play out in relation to you and stopping drinking?

The words you choose to use can be powerful tools that will help you to achieve your goals in this life. They can also be used as weapons against you.

If you want to apply the word alcoholic to yourself, only use it before you quit drinking. I don't think you should use the word to describe yourself once you don't use alcohol any more. It carries too much emotional baggage.

As far as I'm concerned, once I stopped using alcohol, I stopped being an alcoholic. When I quit smoking, I didn't continue to call myself a smoker. Before I stopped drinking, I was technically classed as obese. In the last year, I've lost over 60 pounds. Do I continue to call myself overweight or obese? Of course not! That would be completely ridiculous. It is just as ridiculous to call yourself an alcoholic after you've stopped using the drug.

You are what you think you are!

I really feel sorry for people who have eliminated alcohol from their lives and yet still continue to use the alcoholic label against themselves. I once had a chat with a woman who hadn't drank in over 20 years, not a single drop, yet she still called herself an alcoholic and insisted that one drink would send her back to the beginning again. How sad is that!

Defining Alcoholic

Let's take a look at the word alcoholic.*

An <u>alcoholic</u> is a person *"suffering from alcoholism."*

<u>Alcoholism</u> is *"a **chronic** disorder characterized by **dependence** on alcohol, **repeated excessive use** of alcoholic beverages, the development of **withdrawal symptoms** on reducing or ceasing intake, **morbidity** that may include **cirrhosis of the***

liver, and **decreased ability to function socially and vocationally**." [Emphasis mine]

Most people I know who drink, do so **chronically**, they don't use alcohol once and forget about it. They tend to repeatedly use on a regular basis.

Dependence is characterized as *"the state of relying on or needing someone or something for aid, support, or the like."* Most drinkers use alcohol as a way of relaxing, socializing, partying, etc., and would feel uncomfortable, to say the least, if they couldn't drink at these times, even though most wouldn't admit it.

Many of those people who drink chronically, and are dependent on alcohol, **repeatedly exceed** the recommended daily or weekly use. They also suffer from certain withdrawal symptoms if they reduce or cease their intake. Many would have some difficulty sleeping, feel mildly anxious at times when they would otherwise be using, and some may feel slightly nauseous or sweaty. These are all symptoms of alcohol withdrawal syndrome. They're also symptoms of a bad hangover!

It's estimated that absenteeism and below standard job performance caused through alcohol use, and more specifically hangover, costs an average of $2000 per year for every working adult in the United States, a whopping total of $48 billion every year. I think this could easily be seen as a **decreased ability to function**.

The same report, from the Annals of Internal Medicine, concludes that a hangover "has substantial **morbidity** and societal cost".

There are many derivatives from the word alcoholic, like shopaholic, golfaholic, chocaholic, sugarholic, and foodaholic. Each of these refers to a person who has a bad habit, they shop too much, play too much golf, eat too much chocolate, sugar, or food. I've even heard of curryholics! None of these derivatives has the negative ring that alcoholic does.

Recognizing You Have a Problem

I'm not trying to lessen the seriousness of being an alcoholic. It's a very serious business. What I'm saying is that if you look at the definition of an alcoholic, it can be applied a huge number of drinkers, not just those who realize that they have a problem. In other words, you're not in the minority. You *are* in the minority once you recognize alcohol for what it is - an incredibly harmful and dangerous drug. Most people are blissfully unaware that alcohol is even a drug.

Recognizing that you have a problem is the first step towards change. Once you understand that there is a problem, you can't go back to not knowing.

Normal vs Abnormal

When I told my son that I was thinking of stopping using alcohol, I told him that I thought I was an alcoholic and I felt that alcohol was severely hampering my progress through life. He was completely shocked. No way was I an alcoholic! He said I just needed to cut down on my drinking. Even though he knew how much I drank, he didn't think about it as something abnormal.

Unlike most other drugs, using alcohol is mostly seen as a normal part of our everyday lives. It's only when you stop drinking, or you tell people that you're thinking about stopping drinking, that you're perceived as having a problem.

I think part of the reason for this is because when you 'quit' drinking, you're calling attention to the nature of the beast. By stopping drinking you're putting a spotlight onto a truth about alcohol that most people don't want to hear, that alcohol is a drug, that it can seriously damage your health, or worse - we'll see later how many people die as a direct result of long term alcohol consumption.

Wobbling the Self-Concept

We all carry around a mental picture of who we are, it's known as our self-concept. Your self-concept might be *I'm a straight-talking kind of bloke who likes crazy days at the beach. I love having a few beers and mucking around. I work and play hard!*

Or, *I'm a hometown girl and I'm not really interested in travel. I love meeting up with my girlfriends once a week, we drink a few glasses of wine, and have fun.*

Our self-concept is at the heart of how we perceive ourselves. It tells us who we are, how much confidence we have, what we like and dislike, how we feel, and so on. We live our lives to maintain a certain harmony with our self-concept. It's our most treasured and emotional possession.

When you tell someone that you're getting alcohol out of your life for good, you're putting a wobble into the other person's self-concept. You force them to think their own drinking. Even if they quickly put such silly thoughts out of their heads, the idea still threatens their self-concept. They don't want to see their glass of wine or their bottle of beer as a drug. They don't want to see themselves as drug users.

The self-concept is so jealously protected and deeply ingrained that most people will try anything and go to any lengths to protect and preserve it.

Most people will protect their own self-image by moving the blame for your alcohol problems away from the alcohol and placing it entirely on your shoulders as the drinker. It can't be the alcohol because they 'drink' alcohol without causing themselves any harm (what the eye doesn't see, the heart doesn't grieve over). They can 'control' their drinking, they can take it or leave it, and they only get drunk because they want to - not because they are drinking to get drunk.

So they look at you and think that you must have one of those addictive personalities, or you come from a family with addictive tendencies, or you were born with the 'addiction gene'. It's not the alcohol that's caused your problems; it's you as a person. You are an alcoholic. And everyone knows that once an alcoholic, always an alcoholic. They might even feel sorry for you.

Everything is right with the world once again, the self-concept balance has been restored, and they can carry on their merry way believing what they want to believe.

Alcoholic Prejudice in Action

In my day job, I'm a freelance writer of sorts, writing website articles for whoever will pay me the most money. I came across a job posting in February, 2014. It was for a brand new website looking for long term writers. The pay was really good and most of the articles were about self-help and pop psychology, the *how to* type articles. It seemed like a good opportunity for me, so I applied.

It was over a year since I'd quit alcohol. I'd built the website, alcoholmastery.com, and it was really starting to take off and help people. I was spending a lot of time making new videos and writing about how my life had changed for the better since I stopped drinking. I was really enjoying building the site but it wasn't yet paying any of the bills.

A couple of days after I sent the application, I got an email asking if I'd like to do an interview. Great! I sent the guy some examples of my article writing, told him about the website, and some of my plans for the future.

The interview was going fine. He wanted to know all about my style of writing, how long I'd been writing, what my favorite genres were, blah blah, all the typical interview questions.

He told me he'd taken a look at the site and said that the videos could do with some work (which I knew), but that he thought the content was excellent.

Then, it got weird when he started asking me about my alcoholism. *What alcoholism?* I asked. He said *Well you run a site about your drinking problems...* I told him *I run a site about alcohol problems and some of the content is about the drinking problems I used to have, the ones I don't have any more since I stopped using alcohol!* He said *he didn't want alcohol to get in the way of my work*. I told him again that *I didn't drink alcohol so how could it ever get in the way of my work. Alcohol would have definitely influenced and degraded my work if he'd have talked to me a couple of years previously, but then he wouldn't have known I had a drink problem because I wouldn't have told him!*

I knew where he was going with his *logic*. It was the typical - once an alcoholic, always an alcoholic. Only when you stop using alcohol are you seen to have a problem!!!! I couldn't argue with it. I didn't want to argue with it. I knew the job was gone but I didn't really want to work for the guy anyhow. I stuck through the rest of the interview and hung up feeling really pissed off. He sent me an email a couple of days later telling me they had gone for someone else. I didn't come as a massive shock!

Common Responses to Not Drinking

When I tell people I don't drink, I usually get some fairly common responses. Some people immediately go on the defensive. They might tell me about their own drinking habits, how much they have their drinking under control, or how much they like drinking and couldn't live without it - *Sure, isn't life too short!*

Some look at me with pity. Others view me with suspicion, especially if they're out to get drunk, and I'm the guy who's going to remember everything the next day...Oh shit! I completely understand where they're coming from; I was there myself for most of my alcohol drinking life.

Losing Control

So what do I think about the word alcoholism? Alcoholism isn't a lifelong malady that you'll never overcome. I believe that drinking too much can become a bad habit. But just like any other bad habit, it doesn't happen overnight. It's a dynamic process that we've learned to do over years.

After you've quit drinking alcohol, once you never think about it again, never drink it again, why would you still associate yourself with alcohol in any way, shape, or form? It just doesn't making any sense. Some people will say that even if you still think about drinking, you've still got a problem. We'll talk about this later, but sometimes you can't help thinking about drinking. What matters is how you react, what you do about the thinking is what counts.

Alcoholic and alcoholism are just words, no more, no less. It makes no difference what someone else's definition of alcoholic is. It's the way that you interpret the words and apply those interpretations to yourself that matters the most. I don't call myself an alcoholic because it implies that alcohol still has an influence in my life, and it doesn't. I don't accept that I have a gene that's responsible for my past drinking any more than I accept that my drinking stemmed from some disease or that it has become a disease. If I accept any of those things, I lose control.

To change anything requires first that you believe that the change is possible. Next you have to believe that you can effect the change. You must be sure that it is in your power and your control to make the necessary adjustments that will bring about the overall changes that you want.

Calling yourself an alcoholic, believing that you have a disease that forces you to drink, or that a gene is responsible for your *affliction*, means you're not in control, and you'll never be in control. You'll always be a victim of something else, something outside of your ability, or your discipline, or your self-control, or even your awareness.

Change is going to happen anyway, you need to be the one who's in total control over which direction that change is going to take.

The source for the definitions is dictionary.com.

Your Recovery

"Healing is a matter of time, but it is sometimes also a matter of opportunity."
Hippocrates

Dynamic Recovery

Recovery is another label that has become synonymous with addiction. It's usually referred to as the place you'll end up when you stop drinking... 'in recovery'. The problem is that many people see themselves as being 'in recovery' for the rest of their lives, often calling themselves a 'recovering alcoholic', or a 'recovering addict'.

Recovery is a dynamic process with a beginning, a middle, and an end. No two people are going to go through that same recovery process. For instance, you might have more physical recovery than psychological recovery. Perhaps you've been drinking for a long time and your organs need more restoration. In a nutshell, the recovery process should be:

1. You start recovering once you stop drinking.
2. Your body and mind go through the process of recovery.
3. You're recovered.

Recovery is about change. It's not static. It's about you changing from an alcohol user into a non-alcohol user. You can't touch recovery, taste it, smell it, hear it, or feel it. It doesn't exist as a thing.

Sometimes recovery is seen as a process of restoration. It often implies a reversion back to a previous state, reverting to something or someone you used to be. I drank for the best part of my life and I don't think it's possible to go back to who I was before. I don't want to go back to that person. I'm quite happy moving forward and getting as far away from that person as I can. It was my naiveté and inexperience that led me to use alcohol in the first place. I only want to move forward. I want to learn some of the lessons that I've missed out on because of my choices. I look forward to getting up every day and seeing what life has in store.

We'll look at the recovery process a little later in this book.

The Symptoms and Side Effects Of Quitting Drinking

"The language we use to communicate with one another is like a knife. In the hands of a careful and skilled surgeon, a knife can work to do great good. But in the hands of a careless or ignorant person, a knife can cause great harm. Exactly as it is with our words."
Unknown

Side Effects

Two other words to be cautious about are symptoms and side effects. These words feature heavily in addiction literature. They're words that we generally accept as part of the process of quitting drinking. When we're thinking about quitting, we think about the symptoms and side effects that we might go through. But are they the right words to use?

First, let's take a look at side effects.

Side effects refer to any unexpected results you might experience from doing something. Let's take the example of taking prescription pills for a problem you have with sleeping.

You go to your doctor because you can't sleep. After examining you and asking you some questions, your doctor prescribes course a sleeping pills. You take the pill an hour before you hit the sack, and have no trouble getting to sleep. The next morning, you have unexpected headaches and you feel constipated. These are some of the side effects for you from taking that particular sleeping pill. Most medication has side effects because of the complex nature of our bodies, how our physical chemicals need balance and how everything you take into your body will affect that balance in one form or another.

Symptoms

What about symptoms?

A symptom is a *"phenomenon that arises from and accompanies a particular **disease** or **disorder** and serves as an indication of it."*

Can *stopping* doing something be classed as a **disease**? What about a **disorder**?

When you stop drinking alcohol, you're putting yourself completely out of your comfort zone. You're not used to doing without your crutch, so you will feel dis-eased and your life and you will feel temporarily dis-ordered!

But we think about the words disease and disorder as something to fear. They generally equate to feeling mental or physical suffering, to hospitals, injections, medications, relapses, and so on.

Searching for Answers

When you first start to think about quitting alcohol, it's natural to look for information about what to expect. The future is unknown, but we want to have a good idea about all the possibilities that are facing us. An obvious place to start your own search is on the Internet, through Google, Yahoo, or one of the other search engines. These days, it might be the only place you look, it's very accessible and there's a lot of info.

That's one of the problems with this type of search, the vast amount of information that's available.

For the term *alcohol withdrawal*, there are 3,220,000 pages. For *quit alcohol symptoms*, there are 8,350,000 pages. For *stop drinking alcohol*, there are 22 million pages.

The top results for each of these searches are either medical websites or horror stories from the media. All the medical websites use medical language. There's nothing wrong with medical terminology, except if you're trying to quit and you don't want be half scared to death.

Money First

A second problem with these search results is that they're more commercial now than they've ever before. Google, and the other search engines, are businesses. They exist only to make money. So there's absolutely no guarantee that the pages you're shown haven't paid to appear in that spot.

The primary motivation for many of the companies behind these pages is to drive traffic back to expensive quit alcohol programs, hospital stays, or dry-out clinics. These companies don't want you to think that quitting alcohol is easy. These websites are geared towards giving you the bad news about quitting drinking, emphasizing the bad symptoms and the terrible side effects, while minimizing any knowledge that focuses on your ability to quit on your own.

Some unscrupulous web sites will even go so far as to say that everyone who quits alcohol risks death from 'alcohol withdrawal syndrome'. I won't go into a lengthy explanation here about 'alcohol withdrawal syndrome', suffice to say that it covers every conceivable angle from losing a couple of nights sleep to death.

You Don't Need To Know Everything!

Google also tends to deliver a lot of medical websites for this type of search term. Even the best quality medical websites will emphasize the likely or possible symptoms and side effects that a person might go through when they're quitting. They will generally speak in medical jargon.

This is not in *your* best interests.

Think about it. Why are you trying to get alcohol out of your life? Is it because you're spending too much money on alcohol? Probably! But that's hardly the main reason. Are you just fed up with all the time you're wasting while drinking? Again, very likely, but not the main reason.

Most people stop drinking alcohol because they are feeling more pain than pleasure. What used to be an enjoyable pastime has become a life threatening addiction. The hangovers are getting worse. Dark thoughts about the future are becoming more commonplace. Someone close has probably expressed concern, maybe even going so far as to say that they're no longer willing to tolerate your drinking. Fears about the future, about future ill health, or about premature death will all cause you to feel immediate pain.

Once you feel enough pain, you'll start to think about quitting. Once you have it in your mind as a possibility, you'll start to look at your drinking, and everything that goes with it, in a different light. Maybe for the first time in your life, you'll understand just how destructive your drinking has become. Now, every time you drink, you'll have these thoughts in the back of your mind. Every morning you wake up with a horrible hangover that lingers for the rest of the day; you'll be one step closer to saying *enough is enough*.

Then, one day you decide to look for some information about quitting. If your search on the internet provokes fear about what might be in store, you'll give yourself just enough of an excuse to have a rethink, maybe just enough to alter your resolve to quit.

To step over that starting line, you need as much encouragement as you can get.

The Demon Drink

"The supreme art of war is to subdue the enemy without fighting."
Sun Tzu, the Art of War

Conjuring Up Powerful Enemies

You often hear people talking about the "demon drink," like alcohol has a mind of it's own, and an evil twisted mind at that.

Alcohol is only a liquid. It doesn't have a brain, so it can't think. Without your cooperation it can't make a sneak attack on your body, causing you to get drunk or give you a hangover. It cannot destroy your life or the lives of those around you if it stays in the bottle. You have to put it into your mouth and swallow, over and over, for any of the above to happen.

You might think that calling alcohol *the demon drink* only a joke, that these are only words. But, behind these words are powerful images. When you use terms like demon drink, evil alcohol, or the devil's brew, you increase the power that alcohol has over you.

Devil, demon, and evil conjure up images of fearful beasts, terrible acts of violence, cruelty, and destruction, as well as overwhelming power and influence.

The True Power of Alcohol

Why associate alcohol with these images? Alcohol is no more evil than water. When you go into battle, you should try to weaken your enemy as much as possible. If you visualize alcohol having massive power over you, that's exactly what it will have over you, huge power.

It's the same as giving huge power to the *one* drink. How many times have you heard an 'alcoholic' say, all it takes is one drink to put them right back at the beginning. If that's the way you think, of course all it's going to take is the one drink. You need to treat alcohol for what it is, nothing.

My partner has a glass of wine every evening, often poured by me. From my perspective, the wine is nothing! It's a foul smelling, insipid, poisonous glass of moldy grape juice.

Seeing Past the Lies

I also don't buy into the one glass and I'm back being an alcoholic theory. And that's all it is, a theory. It's not the truth, it's only a maybe. It's not reality until you make it a reality. If you believe it's true, that makes it true, at least from your perspective. And that's all that really counts, your perspective. If you can see past the bullshit surrounding alcohol, why would you ever want to drink another drop, never mind a full glass? The alcohol has no power. It's all in your head!

You are much better served to think about alcohol in terms of how weak it is. I used to visualize what was left of my alcohol habit as the Gollem from the Lord of the Rings. When I thought about my habit, I could see and hear a cowering, incompetent, sniveling, useless, impotent, and scared wretched creature who was slowly dying. It didn't represent the alcohol, but the part of me that still wanted to drink. The part of me that still felt that alcohol could play a constructive role in my life. I took great pleasure in watching this bastard slowly die. Every time I thought about drinking, I'd think of the Gollem. Instead of being fearful, I felt happy. The image would make me smile. *It* would give me the strength, not the alcohol.

Power Yourself Up

There's always going to be alcohol. It's your choice how you think whenever you see others drinking, when billboards and TV commercials try to fill your head, or when you pass the alcohol section in your local supermarket. Do you quickly look away, afraid of what effect just looking at the rows of bottles might have on you? Or do you hold you head up high, puff out your chest, and be proud that none of this propaganda works on you anymore? You can now see the fancy bottles as just tricks on a shelf. The choice is always yours!

Hitting Rock Bottom

"Rock bottom became the solid foundation on which I rebuilt my life."
J.K. Rowling

Where's Rock Bottom?

Do you need to reach rock bottom before you quit drinking?

What's your idea of rock bottom? What does it mean to you? Reaching rock bottom is a place where a person may feel that they have nothing left to lose. It's the place where they've lost everything, their job, family, home, and so on. Rock bottom could mean that they don't have a roof over their head or enough food to keep the hunger at bay.

Every person's 'rock bottom' is going to be different, and it's another example of how damaging language can be.

For me, the images I get when I think of rock bottom is a person who's living on the street. They're hungry all the time, and they don't really care about life or living any more. They have no ambition, no reasons for existing other than where they're going find their next drink, and they make no contribution to anything other than paying for the booze.

Rock bottom means you can't go any further down. Real rock bottom is a pine box at the bottom of a hole in the ground.

Listening and Seeing the Signs on Your Way Down

Most people who quit drinking alcohol, or stop using any drug, never hit rock bottom. Most people cop on to themselves before they get anywhere close.

There are plenty of signs on the way down, all pointing to your need to change. If you honestly open your eyes and take a good look around, you'll have no trouble seeing yours.

The thing is not to wait until you've no choice. Understand that sooner or later the decision has to be made. Are you going to allow your life to sink and keep sinking until the decision to do something is taken out of your hands? Will you wait until a doctor tells you something that will force a change? Will you wait until your partner says they've had enough? Open your eyes and see the signs now, before it's too late.

There's usually one event that pushes a person over the edge. Some people use that event as the springboard to change. For others its still not enough. They need to go deeper.

Your personal bottom is where you choose it to be. All you have to do is to stop digging!

Chapter Four

Fears

"Fear keeps us focused on the past or worried about the future. If we can acknowledge our fear, we can realize that right now we are okay. Right now, today, we are still alive, and our bodies are working marvelously. Our eyes can still see the beautiful sky. Our ears can still hear the voices of our loved ones."
Thich Nhat Hanh

Searching For Answers

As we saw earlier, many people start out on this journey with their fears all stoked up.

The desire to quit is there. They have this great moment of clarity, an understanding that things can't go on the way they've been going, and a desperate need to make changes. Moderation has been tried without success. All it takes is a couple of slips and the old habits come back to the surface. This time, it all feels different. There's a determination that's been absent in all your previous attempts. Things need to be put right, and you have a resolve to persist with whatever it takes to beat this thing.

So you start searching for some answers. Your search might begin online. You talk to people in forums. You search the net looking for answers. You find blogs and medical websites. You look on Wikipedia, Yahoo answers, Quora, Facebook, Twitter, and so on. By the time you've finished, you're in more confusion than when you started. Instead of finding answers, all you've managed to do is stoke your fears more.

What Do We Fear?

Again, quitting drinking is simple. Once you stop putting the alcohol into your mouth, you've done it. The rest is about adjustment. All the fear is in your head.

What do we fear most?

We have fears about the unknown and every part of the future is unknown. You never know what's going to happen around the corner.

We fear change. Our day to day lives are spent well within our comfort zones. This is where we feel "happy." Unfortunately, staying in our comfort zones means we don't change, at least not deliberately. To change anything significantly in this life, we need to burst out of those comfort bubbles.

Changing means discomfort and we don't like discomfort. But getting out of our comfort zone doesn't take much change. You can do it little by little and still see significant results.

We also fear failure. What happens if we go for it balls out and we still fail? What if we tell everyone that we're quitting alcohol for good and we don't manage to do it? What if we make a complete idiot out of ourselves? What if ...?

We fear success even more. What if I successfully quit drinking? What will it be like when I can't have a drink EVER again? What will I do when I have a terrible day and want to commiserate with myself? What will I do when I have a great day and want to celebrate with myself? What if ...?

Affecting Fear

Fear is stoked by your environment. It can even be kicked off by the people around you who are not too happy with your decision. You quitting drinking is making them look bad. They drink as much as you, after all. If you had a problem with the amount of alcohol you were using, so must they! Your efforts open up a stream of thoughts that they would rather suppress, and it's your fault.

Another thing that stokes fear is complication. Unnecessary complexity breeds doubt. The simpler you can make things, the better.

The problem with simple is that it doesn't always mean easy. Most people are not looking for the simple way out, they're looking for the easy way out, the magic bullet. They want to make the decision, go to bed, and have the result magically appear in the morning, like a stocking full of Santa goodies hanging on the end of the bed.

Arriving in the Tomorrow

Life doesn't work in such an easy fashion, as we all know. There's a childish part in each of us that hopes for and pursues the most expedient way of doing things that's possible. We always want something for nothing. No hard work, no waiting long periods of time, we want it here and now. When you get something for nothing, there's always a price to be paid later. That's what we've been doing all along, taking the easy road out of our problems through drinking alcohol. The easy road means that we don't have to think too much about anything negative. It's the one guaranteed way we've always found to stop the thoughts we don't want to think.

Now, we've finally arrived at the place where we have to pay the price for all that thought suppression. Getting out of this situation requires a change in thinking. We have to get away from always putting pleasure first and offsetting the pain until tomorrow. We've already arrived in the tomorrow!

Deep down we all know that nothing worthwhile is easy. Change is going to happen, whether we like it or not. We can make the changes ourselves, like quitting drinking, or we can allow those changes to just happen to us. It's our choice, either way!

Killing Your Determination

Our old fearful selves are saying that we're better off just staying the way we are. We tell ourselves that things are not all that bad. We tell ourselves that all we need to do is get our drinking under control and everything will be just fine. We're sure that things are going to be good because nothing bad will ever really happen to us.

Don't listen to that bullshit. We're the worst predictors of our own future. We predict what we want to happen, not what is realistically going to happen. We predict the future with the thoughts and emotions that we're thinking right now. If you think about the future when you're in a bad mood or in the middle of a depressed moment, your future will almost always look negative. On the other hand, if you imagine the type of future that's in store for you while you're extremely happy, you're outlook will more than likely be much more optimistic.

One of the big problems with fear is that it will kill your determination faster than anything else.

If you start to worry about things before they even happen, before you step over the starting line, there's always an easy fix waiting. All you have to do is go to the pub, to the store, fetch a few cans, or a bottle of your beloved booze, and all your doubts and troubles will be gone, temporarily. You're right back in your comfort zone, and feeling good. What was it you were worrying about again? You're still going to stop drinking, but just not right now. You'll just drink for a few more weeks. You'll definitely quit in January. All the pressure of Christmas will be gone, and you'll be much stronger.

What Do You Want?

The way of avoiding fear is not to fill your head with all the bullshit in the first place. You need to get a grip on *your* reality. What is it you really want in your life? What is it that you're missing out on while you're stuck in the pub with all the other losers? Which of your dreams could you be getting one step closer? Instead, you're on your sofa drinking wine, filling some rich guy's bank account, sipping yourself away from your dreams while making his dreams come true!

I had to ask myself these questions. I had to try and be as honest with myself as I could. What happens when I quit? Will I still be able to mix it up with my drinking mates?

No!!!

Why not?

Because they're all losers who are doing the same loser bullshit that I've been doing for the past 30 years. That's the way I had to see them. They're never going to change. And even if they do, I can't wait for that to happen, I haven't got the time. I have to look after myself.

Life is short, I need to start being a good dad and a good partner right now, I don't have the time to wait anymore. If I want to do it, it's got to be now. I don't have the time to pretend that everything is going to be alright. If I stay in the bar listening to these people, it won't be long before I'm dragged back to where I was, back to the black.

In this chapter, we'll look at some of the most common fears.

Getting over the starting line

The simplest part of quitting drinking is actually stopping doing it. You only need to do this once. You don't have to sweat about eliminating the alcohol from your body or repairing the damage that's been caused; your body will take care of that. You just have to stop putting the alcohol in.

The hardest part of quitting drinking is stepping over that starting line. To do that means you have to make the commitment to yourself and to the people in your life who you love, that you will never, ever drink alcohol again!

The most protracted part of quitting drinking is removing alcohol from your thinking. To remove any thoughts about alcohol is nearly impossible. You can't not think about something. Alcohol is going to pop up in your head every so often, as is drinking alcohol, getting pissed, and all the rest. Don't worry though, there are ways of dealing with this. The biggest impact you will have on your future is by changing the way you think about alcohol and about your relationship with this and every other drug or addiction in your life.

Taking Your First Step

The number one thing that'll stop you from making that commitment and actually taking that first step is your own fear.

It can take a big leap of faith to step over the starting line and often only a small dose of fear to push you back across again. So it's important for you to keep your fear exposure to an absolute minimum.

Fear of Death

"To fear death, gentlemen, is no other than to think oneself wise when one is not, to think one knows what one does not know. No one knows whether death may not be the greatest of all blessings for a man, yet men fear it as if they knew that it is the greatest of evils."
Socrates

One of the biggest fears anyone can have is the fear of dying. Can you really die from quitting drinking?

The hard truth is that some people do die when they abruptly stop consuming alcohol, there's no getting away from that. I'm not a doctor, so I can't tell you what causes this. I can only presume that there are many causes, all related to the amounts of alcohol that you've already consumed, the damage that's already been done to your body, and the internal chemical imbalances that are constantly struggling to readjust.

What Is Your Risk?

The more alcohol you drink the more risk you face once you stop. If you don't drink every day, and on your day's off you don't feel ill (apart from your hangovers), there's nothing worry about. That takes into account about 95% of all heavy drinkers.

If you use alcohol all day, every day, you're chances of going through some severe withdrawal symptoms are a lot higher. Extremely heavy drinkers are at most risk. There are plenty of websites where you'll find long lists of all of these symptoms.

I've tried very hard to come up with some reliable statistics for the numbers of people who die yearly from quitting drinking, but I can't find anything. I would think that death from quitting alcohol would be listed under deaths *caused* by alcohol, not deaths from quitting. I'm not sure though, but it sounds logical. On the other hand, there's a mountain of statistics about the numbers of people who die from *drinking* alcohol.

Fear Tactics

As we've seen, one fear tactic used by the *quit alcohol industry* is to say that no drinker should contemplate quitting on her own, without medical assistance. They play up the risks of death and severe withdrawal symptoms in an attempt to terrorize you into enrolling on one of their treatment programs. I'm not suggesting that the whole quit alcohol industry is like this, but there is a certain element within that industry and they're very vocal and well financed.

And just to put this into perspective, if you are at serious risk of death from quitting alcohol, there's no guarantee that medical attention can do anything for you. Take the case of Ryan Rogers. He was the subject of a documentary made by the National Geographic channel called *Drugged - High on Alcohol*. Rogers had severe alcohol problem. At his worst, he was drinking 3 pints of vodka a day. He started when his father passed away four years earlier. He agreed to get medical help for his habit, but died 17 days into treatment. You can watch the documentary on YouTube.

I'm not suggesting that you shouldn't get help if you need it. People's lives are saved with timely interventions like this. I'm saying that there is absolutely no need to mess your head up with thoughts about dying if you're not at risk. If a person is needlessly worrying about dying, or any of the other severe symptoms that you might never go through, it could very well prevent her from taking that all-important first step. The fear of hearing terrible news might stop her from even speaking with a doctor (See later).

Perspectives on Risk

Life by its very nature involves a lot of risks. There's a chance that you could die simply crossing the road or even walking down the street.

A couple of years ago, there was a woman in her 20s who was killed as she stood on a London street eating a banana. An office building was being refurbished in Central London, which included replacing all the windows at ground level. New windows were delivered to the site and they were so heavy that they had to be lifted from the delivery truck by a heavy duty crane. One of these windows was propped up against a wall when a freak gust of wind caught it and blew it over on top of the young woman. She died on the spot. She was just in the wrong place at the wrong time.

A few weeks ago, as I'm writing this, a young man was killed in our local theme park. He was in Spain on holiday with family and friends. Like many visitors to the area, the group took a day trip to the local theme park. I don't know the ins and outs of the story, but the young lad got onto one of the park's fastest rides, each circuit taking about 45 seconds and involving many high speed twists and turns. As the car he was sitting in spun into one of these turns, the barrier that was supposed to secure him to the seat failed and snapped open. He was thrown out of the seat to his death.

The theme park has been operating for 14 years and this was the first fatality it ever had. The chances of it ever happening again are infinitesimal, a few million to one. I've been on that ride several times and I don't think I'll ever have the courage to get on it again, or any of the other rides for that matter. Why? Because I'm scared, I don't want to die just yet, thanks very much.

Is that logical thinking?

No, not at all!

But that's how the human brain works.

How many people go into hospital for routine operations and never come out again.

It happens all the time!

Some people get allergic reactions to medication, side effects that make them ill. Some of them even die. Does this mean that you should never go to hospital or take medication? Of course not!

There's a risk associated with everything in this life.

Quitting Vs Not Quitting

As I said earlier, there are no easily accessible statistics for problems with quitting drinking alcohol, but there's a mountain of stats for the problems associated with drinking alcohol.

Alcohol consumption is the cause of more than 200 different diseases and injuries. In 2012, 5.9% of total deaths were linked with alcohol use, about

3,300,000 people. Also in the same year, it was calculated that 139,000,000 net years of "healthy" life were lost (Disability Life-Adjusted Years - DALYs). And for young men and women, between the ages of 20 and 39, a massive 25% of all deaths are alcohol related.

These statistics are catastrophic, and they prove beyond all doubt that your risks are far greater if you stay drinking!

Quitting Is about Learning

Quitting alcohol is a learning process as much as it's about beating a bad habit. It's about learning new ways of dealing with your life. In some instances, you'll be relearning old skills. In other instances you'll need to learn new skills, skills you didn't learn when you were younger because you were using alcohol as your tool.

Learning to live your life without alcohol should be approached in a similar way as you'd approach learning any other skill.

Learning about Dangers

Let's say, for instance, I wanted to learn how to swim. I don't like the water because I'm not a very good swimmer. I can swim some lengths of the local pool, but despite living 50 meters from the Mediterranean Sea, I don't swim because I have no confidence in my ability, I've listened to too many horror stories about undercurrents and the like, and I've watched *Jaws* - five times!

If I went for swimming lessons, one of the first things I'd expect to be taught would be how to stay afloat and keep calm. I'd also expect lessons in correct breathing techniques, building my overall strength, different swimming strokes, and so on.

Imagine if I arrived on the first day, all ready to learn this new life saving skill, and the instructor asks us all to gather in a semi-circle beside the pool. Then he says that before we get started on our first lesson, he wants to tell us all that people have died when they have been learning how to swim. He says that more people die on their first and second swimming lessons than during any other swimming lesson. He then goes on to tell us in detail what dying by drowning looks and feels like. No one would even get into the water.

Needing To Know?

Why are we filling the already fearful heads of people who want to quit drinking with all the dreadful things that might never happen? There is absolutely no reason for it. Most people are not susceptible to any terrible side effects of quitting, so why tell them of the possibility? I know there are going to be people who will say that it's your right to know. Is it your right to know that you could be knocked down any time you cross the road. Or your right to know that the airplane you're about to board could fall out of the sky and smash into a million pieces on the ground.

Why do you want to know these things?

What will be, will be.

Take the precautions.

Speak to your doctor.

But above all, make sure you step across that starting line full of confidence in your own ability to quit.

The confidence that you can do it!

Going to Your Doctor

"My doctor gave me two weeks to live. I hope they're in August."
Ronnie Shakes

Many people ask me if I went to see my doctor before I quit. In the interests of full disclosure, I have to say I didn't. For better or worse, I knew what I was letting myself in for and I didn't want to hand over 50 Euro so that my doctor could tell me what I already knew – that I had to quit drinking. Nor did I want his advice about a support group I could attend or which pills I could consider taking if the symptoms got bad.

Regardless of your opinion about my actions, or my motivations for taking those actions, the decision was mine to make. It was my personal choice. I'm not suggesting to anyone that they shouldn't get medical advice before they start on their own journey. My advice to everyone is have yourself checked first.

Proof I Wasn't Going to Die Just Yet

The reason I didn't go to the doctor was because I'd previously quit drinking for almost a year in 2008. I didn't go through any major discomfort, and I obviously didn't die from quitting. Between the time I started back on the alcohol, in November 2008, and when I quit again in 2013, I didn't drink every day.

I wanted to drink every day, it was a big part of my life, but I just couldn't drink all the time. I had to work. I was driving long distances to get to work, and I'd often miss a day or two of drinking just to prove to myself that I could. On the days that I took off, I'd generally feel good, with very little discomfort apart from some persistent cravings for alcohol.

When I didn't drink, my mind would go through a mental tug of war. One side of my mind was insisting that there wasn't a problem in having a drink, the other insisting that it wasn't good to drink every day. It was like a relentless bitching session.

So I was never really in danger from quitting. I'd had plenty of dry days to know that, once I did quit, any battles I faced would be totally in my head. All my risks would only happen if I kept using alcohol. I didn't need a doctor to tell me that home truth.

Drinking Risks vs Non-Drinking Risks

I worked in forestry for a long time. I used chainsaws, wood chippers, forwarders, harvesters, handsaws, sledgehammers, and I was in daily contact with falling trees, flying branches, and crazy squirrels. In all my time working in this environment, I never had an injury, apart from the odd finger cut while I was sharpening my saw.

Almost every injury that I've ever sustained in my adult life has happened when I was drinking alcohol or should I say while I was drunk. I broke my ankle twice jumping over fences while drunk. On both occasions I bent my foot in a way that no foot should be bent. I've slipped and fallen numerous times. I've come off bikes, fallen down hills, and stumbled into ditches.

I've suffered from stomach problems and ulcers because of my drinking. I've had kidney problems, liver problems, and too many hangovers to even count. Drinking alcohol also weakened my immune system, which left me open to all sorts of bugs, flus, and infections.

Alcohol Tolerance

Just because the human body is capable of reducing some of the effects of alcohol by developing tolerances, drinking the stuff is no less dangerous in the end. In fact, tolerance – or your ability to hold your drink – only masks the damage.

Because you're able to drink more without feeling it, you might surmise that your body is developing immunity. The truth is that larger doses of alcohol mean greater damage. The more alcohol you drink, the more alcohol is floating around your system. Tolerance doesn't prevent or reduce damage. All tolerance does is alter the amount of alcohol you can drink without feeling the effects. Just because you don't feel the effects doesn't mean the alcohol is not affecting you. The more you drink, the more you can tolerate, the more damage is being caused. The more you can tolerate, the more you need to drink, and the more damage is caused. It's a vicious circle.

Drunken Fools

Other dangers include putting yourself in compromising situations when you're drunk. Even if you're in the best of health and with all your wits about you, you need to be very careful walking through most city streets late at night. How much more danger is there while you're drunk? How many times I have seen a young man, while he's drunk, picking a fight with a much larger opponent, people running down the middle of the road, jumping on and off things. Many people, young men especially, take part in some very dangerous behavior while they're drunk.

Don't be fooled into thinking that quitting drinking is going to be easy or without its own risks. But the dangers involved in quitting drinking are minute compared to the dangers of continuing down the alcohol path.

Again, if you have any doubts, go see your doctor. You want to step over that starting line with as much confidence as possible. That means eliminating as much negative thinking as possible.

"Symptoms" after Quitting and Making Comparisons

"Confidence is preparation. Everything else is beyond your control."
Richard Kline

There's often a lot of fear associated with the symptoms and side effects that might happen once we stop. It's another irrational fear because we've no idea what's going to happen to us once we step over the line.

It's difficult to make predictions, so your best bet is to keep any future forecasting to a minimum. You don't need to know most of the information that's out about what might happen; most of it won't concern you. But just by reading or listening to too much negativity could manufacture all sorts of reasons in your mind to be concerned! Sometimes, ignorance is bliss!

Keep It Simple!

You don't need to know every symptom, craving or side effect that could possibly affect you. It's what author Wayne Dyer calls the *Woulda, Coulda, Shoulda's* of life. There can only be what *is*! Nothing more! Everything else is nonsense or speculation at best.

If you visit your doctor because you've got a pain in your belly, will she tell you all the possible causes? Does she go through the side effects of each medication she prescribes? Does she tell you every conceivable symptom that you should steel yourself against?

NO!

Why not?

To begin with, she doesn't have the time. Second, she knows that the more she tells you about these things, the more likely you are to experience the symptoms and side effects as a result. This is because your thoughts and emotions can get all twisted up and can affect you physically. Sometimes thinking about a "symptom" is all it takes to create the symptom. Every hypochondriac knows this.

Your doctor will tell you the bare minimum you need to know. Get lots of rest, take time off work, take these pills, and drink plenty of water. She will only explain the things that will benefit you.

Sticking to the Controllable

It's the same with quitting alcohol. Don't listen to or read up on every little thing that could go wrong or might go wrong. Stick to concentrating on the positives. Focus on those things that you can control, on the things that will help you in making your adjustments.

In my YouTube videos, I hate talking about the possible symptoms or side effects. Que sera, sera! What will be, will be. You'll know exactly what you'll feel when you feel it, not a moment sooner. So don't torture yourself unnecessarily.

I love speaking about the mountains of shit that can happen to you if you don't quit. I love to talk about sagging heart muscles, scarred and necrotic livers, and wet brain – or Wernicke-Korsakoff syndrome – an often irreversible form of brain damage affecting memory, intelligence, and information processing.

I love talking about the worst visions I had of my alcoholic future. How I used to visualize my son's face as he stood over my alcohol poisoned sick body.

I love talking about those things because there's a positive purpose to explaining them. If I can get a person to think about the dangers to their health, the tragedy of relationships lost, or the selfish destruction of one human life, it might bring them one step closer to crossing their own starting line and never looking back.

Comparing "Is" with "Might Be"

One of the things that will often prevent people from crossing that starting line is the fear of what *might* happen. That fear could be about not having alcohol in your life any more, not having a crutch to fall back upon, or just how much pain are you going to go through as part of the withdrawal process.

A good idea is to make some comparisons between what *is* happening in your life right now and what *might* happen once you quit.

Examine the pain that you are in right now, the pain that's causing you to think about quitting. Think about every area in your life that's been touched by your alcohol use. These are the thoughts that will force you to confront this creeping destruction, perhaps for the first time in your life. They are the thoughts that will give you the motivation to push through any tough moments that you might go through in the days and weeks ahead.

Always Being the Drunk

For me, I couldn't face living the rest of my life being *the* drunk at every occasion. I was feeling a lot of pain about how I was acting in front of my

...... How could I feel pride in myself when I was contributing toward his alcohol habits! I've always tried to be a great role model to my son, but I knew that by drinking this way, I was being a terrible example. Even though I felt I was a great dad in many other areas of my life, drinking alcohol totally let me down, and let him down.

My health was really starting to suffer. The more I drank, the worse the hangovers were getting. Sometimes, they were lasting more than a couple of days. Even drinking to cure the hangover wasn't helping anymore; it was barely taking the edge off. When I woke up after a big drinking session, I felt like I was dying, literally. I imagined that if I kept using this drug, I'd eventually need to drink in the morning, just to feel normal.

I knew that whatever it took to get over this bad habit had to be better than what I was going through each and every day. And I was right! My symptoms were nowhere near what I had imagined they would be like.

You Are Here

If you feel afraid of crossing the line, spend some time thinking about where you are now. Look at how bad your hangovers are getting. Understand that they're never going to improve. The more you drink, the worse your hangovers will become.

Think about your health. How much has it deteriorated over the last few years? Think about your relationships. How have they been affected? Think about as many aspects of your life as you can.

Once you do that, you are in a good place to start making comparisons.

The Symptoms and Side Effects of My Drinking!

"Only two things are infinite, the universe and human stupidity, and I'm not sure about the former."
Albert Einstein

Sleeping With the Enemy

My drinking was definitely taking the best out of me. I don't think I'd had a sound sleep in years, not since I'd quit the last time. Most nights were about hitting the pillow and being comatose very quickly, or if I didn't drink, tossing and turning for what seemed like hours, waiting for sleep to come.

When I got into bed drunk, my body felt like it was completely shutting down. It was like flicking a switch and all the lights going out. It was the most efficient way that my body had of dealing with the poison that I kept drinking. Knock out the idiot, only keep the essential life support ticking over, and then get to work on damage limitation.

I'd nearly always wake up after 4-5 hours of so-called sleep. I'd lay there, feeling like crap, my head buzzing, my body ill, listening to the BOOM BOOM BOOM that felt like heart was trying to hop out of my chest, my head banging to the same insane rhythm. My mouth felt like I hadn't drunk in weeks, despite the gallons of beer I'd swigged the night before. Completely dehydrated and needing to hold onto as much liquid as possible, the diuretic effect of the alcohol would continue sending the wrong signals to my kidneys ... get rid of more water. My bladder would be only too happy to oblige.

Every organ in my body seemed to ache. Everything gets screwed up with alcohol poisoning, or the hangover, as we like to call it. The body is under immense pressure to eliminate the poison and everything else gets either no look in, or half-assed attention at best.

Payback

Once I woke up, I'd always find it hard getting back to sleep again. The numbing effect of the alcohol had all but disappeared and now it was time to pay the cost.

If I managed to get back to sleep, I'd only be delaying the inevitable sickness by a couple of hours of sporadic rest. Usually, sleep was gone. I'd have to get up so as not to wake my soundly sleeping partner.

I'd spend the day in a sort of twilight zone. I wouldn't, or couldn't work! Feeling sorry for myself was my default state of mind. Sorry for drinking so much. Sorry for feeling so bad. Sorry for me! I'd be curled up on the couch, in front of the computer, or just sitting on the balcony staring into space. It all amounted to the same thing ... doing as little as possible, achieving nothing, and letting the day slowly seep away!

Most of my hangovers were taking two or three days to clear. The fact is I never allowed them to completely clear up because by the time the evening came, I was drinking again. At best I'd wait until the next day. I was on a continuous cycle of drink - drunk - detox - drink - drunk - detox - and on and on - forever spinning around and around.

The hangovers felt like I had the flu. Nausea, sometimes vomiting, very sweaty, headaches, aches throughout my body, kidney pain, liver pain, joint pain. Brain dead! Staring into space like a zombie. At least zombies have ambitions, even if those ambitions are fairly obsessive. My ambitions were to get to tomorrow as fast as possible. My brain felt like it was wrapped in a wet towel, but without any of the soft comfort.

Before and After

Now I'm in a position to make comparisons between before and after. All the symptoms and the side effects and the cravings, all the unpleasantness, all the discomfort that I went through in the first few days after I stopped poisoning myself, were all a walk in the park compared to how I was feeling before!

It took time for my body and brain to adjust. It took time for the alcohol to be eliminated completely from my system. But it wasn't long before I was feeling physically good. I knew that once I stopped, I'd have to go through one last hangover, completely through it this time, no matter how long it took. As I've said, my hangovers were starting to last a few days.

I often look back to that first video I made for Alcohol Mastery, Video Journal 1. It was made one week after I quit. Every time I watch it, I'm reminded of who I used to be. It's a snapshot of what my life looks like when I'm drinking. I see the bloated and ill guy that I remember so well. The first time I replayed the video, the thing that immediately struck me was the sadness in my eyes.

It's a place to which I'm never going back.

My Quit

"I don't seek discomfort. But, very often, you realise that what you fear is actually quite ephemeral; something's different, something's unfamiliar; therefore, it must be worse."
Michael Palin

Finding Pink Elephants

Before I quit, whenever I thought about the idea of never having a drink again, or more aptly how I was going to feel in those first few days, I felt like I was going to go through hell. I'd read a lot of the usual crap on the web. The truth is, I lapped it up. I had it in my head that there was no turning back for me now and I was determined to see this process through. I wanted to know everything there was to know about quitting. By the time I'd finished my online reading, I was sure I was going to see little pink elephants and have visions of demons and imps.

I'd quit drinking a few years ago and I couldn't remember going through many side effects back then. I had another few years drinking under my belt at this stage and this time I didn't think I was going to get away with it so easily. Thankfully, I was wrong.

Despite winding myself up, the only real "symptom" I experienced was difficulty sleeping. I also felt a little shakiness, but most of that was due to being rattled by all the boozing. All I was experiencing, in those first few days, was just going through my bog standard hangover.

Finding Sleep

My sleep difficulties lasted about a month. Or I should say it took about a month to go from hardly any sleep to having a great sleep and feeling entirely rested when I woke in the morning.

The first few days were the most challenging. Reading has always been a big part of my bedtime routine. It could sometimes prove difficult or impossible to read while I was drinking, the first law of reading is to be able to see the words. My normal ritual was to have a few drinks in the evening until I felt tired. Then I'd get into bed, open a book, read two or three paragraphs, and I'd be away to la la land!

In those first few days after I quit, my bedtime routine was missing one essential element, the alcohol. I would read, and read, and read. My eyes would get heavy, I'd put down the book, ready for sleep, and as soon as I turned out the light I'd be wide awake again. This pattern would continue for a couple of hours until I eventually dropped off into a kind of fitful rest. You couldn't really call it sleep.

Gradually, as my body got used to the idea that no more alcohol would be forthcoming, falling asleep got easier and easier. It still took a few more practice runs without alcohol before I was able to stay asleep for more than a few hours, but I got there in the end. For the first time in a very long time, I was getting a complete rest every night. Even my dreams came back. I had dreams when I was using alcohol, but those dreams were like I was viewing them with my head stuck in a fish bowl. Most of the time, I couldn't even remember what they were about. Now I was having proper vivid dreams, good dreams that I liked and wanted to remember.

The Battle for Mind

The battle of my mind took a bit longer. I shouldn't call it a battle because I was enjoying it. As you'll see, most of my effort would not go into wondering how I would ever survive without alcohol; it was how I'd fill the vacant gaps that were left in my daily life. I used to drink a lot. I drank most evenings and every weekend. Now I had to fill those empty spaces without going mad!

Finding Perspective

"When you can imagine you begin to create and when you begin to create you realize that you can create a world that you prefer to live in, rather than a world that you're suffering in."
Ben Okri

You Are Here

How do you find the courage to cross that line? How do you minimize the fear and maximize your resolve and determination to take that first step? I believe you do these things by first getting a firm handle on *your* perspective. You have to understand where you are now and how you got here. You can't know where you're going unless you know from where you're starting.

More importantly, you need to look at both possible futures that are waiting for you. We looked at one aspect of this earlier, making your comparisons between your before and after. From another perspective, what future awaits you if you keep drinking? And, what future awaits you once you stop drinking?

Visualize Your Future

A very helpful way of looking at your future is through visualization. Try to imagine yourself as your future self. See and feel what it's like to be the "*you*" of ten years into the future. Look at the people that you care about and how they're acting toward you. Look at your future self from many different angles.

- How much are you drinking?
- How often?
- What is that drinking costing you?
- How is your family life being affected?
- What about your job or business?
- What kind of financial problems are you having?
- How do you fit in your community?
- How is your health affected?

The Immortal Alcoholic

A couple of months before I quit, I found a website called The Immortal Alcoholic. The blog is written by a lady who is long term caring for her husband, an end-stage alcoholic. In one particularly poignant post, she describes what an alcoholic death looks like. She recounts walking into her husband's room. He's lying in a bed, ill, frail, and almost childlike. He can hardly speak, let alone move. In the post she recounts, "There is an odor about him that is so distasteful that it makes me back up when I get near him and couldn't approach him because of the smell."

That one sentence hit me hard. The person she was describing could be the future me! The thought of trying to comfort someone you love, but you can't get close enough to hug them or care for them because they smell so bad. It's a scene that I'd later use to great effect in my own visualizations.

When we're talking about a binge drinker, a heavy drinker, or an alcoholic, we're not talking about someone who's suffering from Alzheimer's or Parkinson's disease. This "disease" is completely self-inflicted. It's a condition that can be prevented. Every drink this person took throughout his life, every selfish mouthful, has led him to a place where he no longer can look after himself. That dirty job is left to someone else, to a caregiver, to this woman. I felt so sorry for her. For him, I felt only anger.

Making Me Think

Linda, the author of The Immortal Alcoholic, may be waiting for the inevitable to happen with her husband. But I want her to know that she made a difference to me. Her story made me see things from a completely different perspective. Her posts forced me to look at my alcohol use objectively, from the context of a selfish addiction. For the first time, I began to examine how my drinking would affect the people I love; not in terms of being drunk, acting stupid, or wasting my life, but in terms of having to take care of my future self. Would they be there for me? Would they care? Could they stick around? Would I want to force that decision on them?

In my visualizations, I imagine what it's like for my son to see me in this same condition. I visualize him coming into my room and I am very ill. I see his face as he tries to get close to me. He's trying to hide his disgust at how badly I smell. As I look into his eyes from my sick bed, I feel the full shame and disgust at how I've let myself drift into this state. I think back to how he used to look up at me when he was a little boy, those big blue eyes and curly blond hair, giving me so much trust, and so much love. In that child's eyes, I can do no wrong. Yet here I am, stinking up the place and killing myself slowly.

Even now, writing this, I feel the emotional bang as that movie plays in my mind. The imagination is a very powerful tool.

Glimpses of Your Future

Your mind is your greatest ally. You should use it to conjure up your own "what if" scenarios of your future. See the inevitable result if you continue poisoning your body. At the same time, realize that it's never too late to change. Facing your future in this way could very well save your life. It won't cost you anything except maybe a few tears.

When you visualize this possible pain in your life for all it's worth, when you force yourself to confront the end result of your drinking, you give yourself a very forceful and long lasting motivation to change. You'll find it very difficult to ignore these visualizations once you've visualized them.

Take yourself on a journey like the one Scrooge had in A *Christmas Carol*. Visualize where you've come from, who you used to be, see the person who used to smile and jump and laugh. See that person whose life didn't revolve around booze and getting drunk. Now see your present life. See yourself truly for what you are now. No bullshit! How are you wasting your precious years getting wasted on a drug? Finally, take yourself on that trip into your future, and see how it all ends!

It won't take long. We're talking about moments. These can be the most important moments you've ever spend in your life.

A Year and a Half through My Journey

"Regret is the worst human emotion. If you took another road, you might have fallen off a cliff. I'm content."
William Shatner

How Did I Get Here?

In the first few months after I'd quit alcohol, I would often ask myself *How did I ever get into that state*?

After a year and a half, I'm getting a better understanding.

As we grow up, we've no real concept of the dangers involved in drinking alcohol. We're taught to look left and right when we cross the road. We're taught which are the highest mountains and the longest rivers in the world. We're taught about history, economics, religion, philosophy, and geography. We're taught not to take sweets from strangers, not to spit, swear, to tuck in our shirts, and to have respect for our elders.

Missing Lessons

We're also taught not to mess with drugs. We learn that drugs are dangerous, drugs are for losers, and drugs will ruin our lives!

At the same time, we teach our children that drinking alcohol is normal. We do teach them that they must wait until they're all grown up before they can partake, but that once we are all grown up, there are really no rules ... except don't become an alcoholic.

This is not surprising because alcohol users are everywhere. They are the politicians who make the rules. They are the police and judges who enforce those rules. They are the businessmen who make the drinks and the doctors and nurses who treat the drunks. And they are the professors and the teachers who educate and guide our children.

Our Fantasy World

Our children live in a world where the Bogeyman, Santa Claus, the Tooth Fairy, and the Easter Bunny are very much real; where the alcoholic is the dirty man in the dirty coat who sleeps in on the dirty ground in the shop doorway.

We live in a world where some drug dealers and drug users are evil scumbags who deserve nothing better than to be locked up, while other drug dealers and drug users (those that deal in and use alcohol) are held up as paragons of virtue and taste, deserving only the best that life has to offer.

By the time our children become adults, by the time they legally can purchase alcohol, we may have taught them how to be careful when drinking. We might tell them not to drink on an empty stomach, to keep away from shorts, and never, ever drink and drive. But we fail to tell them the biggest lesson of all: that alcohol is a drug, just like all those other drugs about which we told them to be careful!

It's a Drink!

We fail in this because, even though it is a drug, and one of the most harmful, *we* don't classify it as a drug. If it's not classified as a drug, even though it has all the hallmarks of a dangerous drug, how can it *be* a drug?

As a consequence, our children will only preserve the illusion. If they get into trouble because they're drinking too much, they're given the advice to moderate, to act responsibly. This advice only serves further to normalize alcohol use.

Moderation and responsibility are not advice you'd give about drug use to a heroin user or a cocaine user. But alcohol is not a drug, like heroin or cocaine, it's only a drink. What could be more normal, even natural, than taking a drink?

And as we've seen, it's only when you hold your head above the parapet and say you're going to quit that you're seen as having a problem. Not before you've quit ... during all that time when you were putting poison into your body, only now that you've stopped.

Trouble Just Arrived

One day you wake up and you realize that you have a problem with alcohol. You see that you're an alcoholic, or whatever you want to call it. You're in trouble and you don't really understand how you got there.

Each bad alcohol habit has been built up by drinking one mouthful at a time. That's how it works. You drink one mouthful after another. You have one drunken night after another. You drink one weekend after another. Soon, you're drinking almost every night. Then you *are* drinking every night. Then you start to drink during the day; then earlier and earlier in the day. Finally, you just can't face life without drinking alcohol.

Telling the Truth

What would happen if everyone was told the truth before they started drinking?

If you knew that you were taking a drug, would you have acted with more caution? Would the adults around you have acted with more responsibility before giving you your first drink?

If you knew alcohol was a drug, just like heroin, cocaine, angel dust, or crack, and that by taking this drug you would be a user, just like any other drug user, and that you had a chance of getting addicted to this drug, just like any other drug, would you have acted with more caution?

If you knew alcohol was a drug, would you still use it in front of your children?

Now you know that alcohol is a drug, at least you know what you're dealing with.

Breaking Habits

One of the vital lessons that I've learned, since I stopped drinking alcohol, is that it's just a bad habit. The internal processes that built your habit are the same processes that will break your habit. Breaking any habit boils down to making adjustments and creating a new set of rules. It'll take time, it will cause discomfort, but it's only one small adjustment after another.

Change is going to happen, whether you like it or not, whether you control it or not. Instead of letting it happen *to* you, you get to push the change in the direction that you want it to go.

The Drinking Disease

"There are two primary choices in life: to accept conditions as they exist, or accept the responsibility for changing them."
Denis Waitley

It's A Control Thing

Treating this habit as a disease is taking the control completely out of your hands.

If you believe it's all in the genes, and that you just happen to be one of the poor souls who were born with the "addiction gene" or the "alcohol gene," you are screwed from the get-go.

How do you ever get rid of a gene from your body and start again? You can't! You're doomed to have this anchor around your neck for the remainder of your life.

What happens if you choose to see this, or any addiction, as a bad habit?

What if you see that it's your thoughts and your behavior that got you into this shit in the first place, and it's your thoughts and behavior that's going to get you out of it again?

Your Ability To Respond

If you look at your drinking this way, there is no blame, there is only responsibility.

The word "responsible" consists of two words, "response" and the suffix "-ible" or "-able". It means your ability to respond.

How can you respond to having an alcohol problem, an alcoholic addiction, or an alcohol habit if it's a disease or if it's in your genes?

Where is your ability to respond?

If you have a disease, surely you're not able to respond. It's a disease; it's beyond your control. Many people go through life looking at things from this perspective. Instead of looking for areas where they can actively make changes, in either their behavior or their environment, they only look for areas where they can alter how they see things. They go through life with the thoughts - It's beyond my control. It's a disease and I can't help it. That's just the way things are!

On the other hand, if you don't have a disease, if it's a habit that you've helped to create, then with the right set of tools you can unmake that habit. You're in complete control and that's the best place to be!

Chapter Five

Recovery

"Tomorrow is the most important thing in life. Comes into us at midnight very clean. It's perfect when it arrives and it puts itself in our hands. It hopes we've learned something from yesterday."
John Wayne

The Recovery Process

We spoke about recovery a bit earlier in this book. Before we delve deeper into what recovery is, here's a quick recap of what we've learned so far.

Recovery is not the place or state you'll be in after you've stopped drinking. It's not a place where you'll remain for the rest of your life.

Recovery is a dynamic process of healing, much like the process you go through when you've broken a bone, but in this case it includes psychological recovery. It's a process with a beginning, middle, and an end.

In the next couple of sections, we'll go through the two types of recovery that are linked to quitting drinking, as I see them. First, we'll look at the day-to-day recovery that all heavy drinkers must go through in order to survive. Then we'll take a look at breakout recovery, the processes your body and mind will go through once you've stopped the flow of alcohol.

Cyclical Recovery

"Do something today that your future self will thank you for!"
Unknown

Never Ending Cycle

Cyclical recovery is the process your body and mind goes through every time you take alcohol or any other drug into your body. As long as you're a user, your body is stuck in this never-ending cycle of intoxication and recovery.

As long as you have alcohol floating around your body, your defenses are permanently switched on.

Our culture may look upon alcohol as a way of getting drunk, having fun, or getting a buzz. Your body only sees the alcohol in one way, as a poison, as something to eliminate as quickly as possible.

As soon as alcohol enters your bloodstream, and for as long as it stays in your body, your defenses will try to limit how far the toxin can travel, reduce the overall damage caused by the toxin, and transform or eliminate the toxin from your body.

Liver Capability

The human liver can only physically handle one unit of alcohol per hour. That's the size of a small glass of wine or half a pint of beer. It's not very much. But in terms of normal levels of alcohol, the types of alcohol found in nature, one unit of alcohol per hour is more than enough.

Your liver has evolved to deal efficiently with the naturally occurring alcohol that is produced inside your body through normal processes such as digestion. It can also deal with most alcohols that are naturally found in the environment like the small amounts of alcohol found in overripe fruits, and so on.

Your liver hasn't evolved the ability to handle the huge doses of toxins to be found in commercially produced alcoholic drinks.

Resting Your Liver

If you're a heavy drinker, your liver never gets a real break. As soon as it gets to work dealing with the first unit, a second arrives, then a third, and so on. There's no staging or holding area where all the incoming alcohol is stored temporarily, waiting patiently to be processed. Your mighty liver has no choice but to allow the overload to flood your network of veins and arteries, saturating your system from your feet to your brain.

Any amount of alcohol in your body is seen as poisoning. In medical terms, alcohol poisoning doesn't happen until the levels of the toxin become so great that normal bodily functioning cannot be maintained.

If you use alcohol every day, does your liver ever get to rest? Does it ever get the chance to concentrate completely on normal filtering processes?

Not really for the heavy drinker! The process of alcohol toxin elimination is constant. It's like a never ending cycle.

Constant Damage Limitation

"Healing doesn't mean the damage never existed... it means that the damage no longer control our lives."
Unknown

When I was drinking alcohol, especially in the latter years, there was always alcohol in my body, even if I hadn't drunk it for a couple of days. My body was in constant damage limitation mode. Being in this state means the body is unable to repair or renew sufficiently because it has to focus on dealing with the incessant flow of alcohol.

If I stopped drinking for a couple of days, maybe my body thought that it was finally getting a handle on things. Then I'd start drinking and the cycle would be triggered again. Drink - Recover - Drink - Recover - Drink - Recover - Drink ...

Then I Really Stopped Drinking

Once I stopped drinking for good, for the first time in a long while my body was able to move past the cyclical recovery. My recovery drive kicked in and started tackling the underlying damage that had been caused by many years of alcoholic assault.

Think about the condition your body must be in after all these years of consistent heavy drinking. Your defense system has had to deal with the regular flood of alcohol toxins that you've thrust upon it, as well as taking care of the day to day contamination that's part of the natural world, from the air, your food, your fingers, and so on.

Suddenly, the alcohol stops. You've taken one last binge and finally you decide that enough is enough!

At Last

Your body doesn't know that the toxic tap has been turned off permanently. It goes through the same motions that it's gone through a thousand of time in the past. It deals with the toxins at one unit per hour as normal, breaking them down, and spitting them out. You go through the same hangover feelings that you've gone through time and again.

This time it's different because the flow never restarts. Your repair system can finally put all its energy into cleaning up the last dregs of alcohol from your system. Once the final mop-up has been completed, your repair system can concentrate fully all its resources on repair and regeneration.

It won't take very long before you start to feel the difference, and this is only the beginning. The best part is you don't have to do a thing. It all takes place behind the scenes, while you're sorting out your head, while you're sleeping, and while you're planning for your bright future.

Breakout Recovery

"Responsibility is the price of freedom."
Elbert Hubbard

Freedom

Once you get over the initial hangover, you're probably heading into territory you haven't seen in a long time. I'd been in that recovery cycle for over five years. In that time, I don't think I ever went more that 2 or 3 days without my fix. Breaking out of that cycle felt fantastic.

This breakout recovery process is not an alcoholic limbo that you'll be stuck in for the rest of your life. It kicks off as soon as you stop drinking and it chugs along, below the surface, until you've recovered.

Your body will finally function as it's supposed to function.

Recovered

There's no magic pill that will accelerate the process. It might take a few weeks, or maybe a few months, before things are operating at normal levels. You will get there. You will find yourself recovered.

From now on, your life should be about building a better version of yourself, one that can achieve the things you want to achieve in this life, not one that's being held back by drugs. It's a steady process that must run its course. However, you can help the process along by providing the right fuel.

Fuelling Your Body's Capacity to Heal

"If we could give every individual the right amount of nourishment and exercise, not too little and not too much, we would have found the safest way to health."
Hippocrates

Fuel 1: Self-Belief

Most of the healing and rebuilding will happen below your awareness. What you can do to help that healing and rebuilding is to provide your body with the right types of fuel for the job.

I know it sounds corny, but the first type of fuel is self-belief. You must believe that your body is capable of making these changes. After all the shit you've put your body through in the past, you're still alive. That is a testament to your body's inner strength. One of the biggest barriers to change is not having the belief that you can effect a change or maintain the changes once you've begun the process. Your body has evolved to be strong. As you already know, your body can put up with all kinds of abuse. You need to maintain your mental strength to help your body; which brings us onto the next fuel.

Fuel 2: Nutrition

If you quit drinking and only feed yourself a diet of McDonald's hamburgers and Coke, you'll be hindering the whole process, not helping. "You are what you eat" may be a cliché, but it's very true. If you eat burgers and fries and Coke, that's what you're going to be made of. The food that you put into your mouth ends up being the building blocks that your system will use to rebuild, to repair, to think, and to act. Do you really want to be made from burger "meat," fries, and sugar water? Is that what you deserve? It's certainly not what your body needs.

Your body needs plenty of fresh, clean water. It needs a diet that's rich in natural whole foods like fruits and vegetables, complex carbohydrates like whole grain bread, whole wheat pasta, or brown rice. It needs proteins that can be found in meat, vegetables, fruit, nuts, grains, or beans. If you eat meat, stick to the leaner cuts to avoid too many bad fats. You should also take a multi-vitamin supplement in the early days. Consider this as a bit of insurance that you're really getting everything that you need.

How quickly your body heals depends a lot on the fuel on which it runs. That fuel is made up of the raw ingredients you put into your body.

Fuel 3: Exercise

The third type of fuel is exercise. Exercise revs you up. If you mix exercise with the other two fuels, good thoughts and good food, you'll have more energy and improve your overall mood.

I always feel better on the days I exercise than on the days when I don't bother. Even if I feel like crap in the morning when I get out of bed, once I get out into the open air and start walking, keeping it up for an hour or two, I always feel better, always! It's the same in the evening. I can have had the most draining day ever, I can be feeling completely exhausted, but if I get out of the house and take a quick walk it makes me feel better, every time. It re-energizes me.

Exercise will help your body to recover. It just helps everything work better and more efficiently. It can help your mind to remain focused and to avoid thinking about the negative aspects of quitting drinking. Oh, and don't forget your rest days. You need those as well.

The Vigorous Cycle

These three elements - self-belief, nutrition, and exercise - are a complete formula for helping your body to repair, rejuvenate, and ultimately maintain a healthy balance throughout your life. Each part of the formula adds fuel to a simple vigorous cycle. By nurturing your self-belief, eating well, and getting your butt up and moving, you're helping to accelerate your recovery.

In the long term, these simple steps will help you to achieve a much more fulfilled life. Your thoughts will be way more positive because your mind is being fueled by the proper food and healthy doses of oxygen from your workouts. You'll make better choices about food and exercise because you're thinking is now much clearer. And you have the energy and stamina to maintain your workouts because you're strengthening your thought patterns and eating the right types of food.

The Body in Balance

"Man maintains his balance, poise, and sense of security only as he is moving forward."
Maxwell Maltz

How Long Does Recovery Take?

One of the most frequent questions asked on the website is *How long will my recovery take?* There's no real answer to this. It'll take as long as it takes. It depends on so many different factors, including how much time and effort you're willing to put into your fueling.

Your body loves balance. It wants nothing more than to run like a well-oiled machine. Some days you feel great, other days you don't feel so hot; but, in general, there's a set-point around which your body thrives. This process is called homeostasis. Even when you're fully dependent on drugs, your system will still try to find a balance.

Once you quit drinking, it's almost inevitable that you'll be uncomfortable for a while. The physical discomfort comes from different areas and no two people are going to go through the same experiences. There will be a lot of changes happening in your body, of that there's no doubt, and a lot of changes happening to your mind. But, because we don't like change it's inevitable that we're going to go through some discomfort.

Balance Restoration

Your system wants to restore balance as soon as possible. We humans are wired for a time and place that has long disappeared. Our primal instincts and abilities have been honed over millions of years to protect ourselves and our families against the fangs and claws of large predators.

You can't run or you can't protect yourself from a saber-toothed tiger if your basic balances are out of whack. Even though we no longer have anything to fear from large predators – we're the hunter instead of the hunted – our systems are still geared to operate under those conditions and with those threats being imminent. From a pure survival point of view, your body needs to restore healthy and balanced levels as soon as possible.

My Own Worst Enemy No More

Before I quit, everything felt like it was exhausted. I was in pain, I was overweight, and I felt chronically ill. After I stopped, it took a while before things got back into balance again. My liver pains were one of the first things to go, probably because the swelling went down. Obviously there were no more hangovers, which was very welcome.

I definitely helped the process along because I had the attitude that I wasn't going to give in this time, no matter what happened. I was determined to get alcohol out of my life permanently, to rebuild my life into something about which I could be proud, and above all to be a great role model to my son. I changed my diet to include a lot more whole foods and eliminated a lot of the junk. I had slip-ups on the way, but that's part of the journey. The main thing always has been to stop being my own worst enemy. I understand now that if I want to have a happy, healthy, and self-fulfilled life, I have to pay the price up front, not somewhere down the line.

Your Body Immigration Officers

"Garbage in garbage out"
George Fuechsel

You Are What You Eat!

Here's one of the best explanations of the maxim *"you are what you eat"* that I've ever come across. This from an Indian spiritual teacher called Sri Swami Satchidananda. You can watch the video here.

He talks about the three monkeys: see no evil, hear no evil, and speak no evil. If we think about our bodies as a country, he says, the senses can be thought of as immigration officers.

These immigration officers are waiting to check everything that comes in to your country.

Your eyes are your first immigration officer. When you want to take a drink of water, your eyes will look over the water and say, "*Yeah, it looks clear. It doesn't look like there's any dirt in it, that's okay to drink."*

Then the water is passed to the next immigration officer, your nose, which is conveniently placed just over your mouth. Anything that wants to go into your mouth must first pass under the scrutiny of this strong sense. So you pass the glass of water under your nose and you smell it; it smells good, it doesn't smell bad, so all is good. It passes the second test.

The mouth is the third immigration officer. You sip the water and roll it around inside your mouth, having a good taste. It tastes good, it tastes like water should taste. Then you swallow it.

Once it passes the taste test, it flows down your throat where it meets the ultimate immigration officer, your stomach.

The Guru talks about how we try to fool our senses into accepting things that shouldn't be put into our bodies. We add colorings to fool the eyes. We add flavorings to fool the nose and the mouth. But the ultimate immigration officer, your stomach, is not fooled by any of these things.

Your First Alcoholic Drink

Take the case of alcohol. When you first drink, you won't go for strong liquors or drinks that demand an acquired taste. You'll go for fruit-based drinks or you'll add something sugary or fruity to the alcohol before you knock it back. So your eyes are fooled into thinking that you're drinking something delicious because it looks familiar. Your nose and mouth are fooled because it smells and tastes like something familiar.

You swallow and it lands in the domain of the fourth immigration officer. You can't fool the stomach. *No, you don't belong here*, and he kicks it out of the country.

If you think back to the beginning, how much of a conscious effort did it take for you to get through your first drinking session? How many times did you feel like vomiting in those early drinking years? Do you remember the spinning sensation when you were drunk, like the whole world was whirling around like a crazed dervish?

This isn't complicated stuff. This is the same advice that's been passed down through hundreds of generations. We all know this already. You don't need a complicated celebrity diet to lose weight, we just need to eat less and exercise more. We don't need anyone to tell us how to stop drinking, we just stop doing it!

The Psychological Aspects of Quitting Drinking

"The law of harvest is to reap more than you sow. Sow an act, and you reap a habit. Sow a habit and you reap a character. Sow a character and you reap a destiny."
James Allen

Dealing with the Mind

As we've seen, the body is pretty much going to take care of the physical part of quitting alcohol. And you can accelerate that process by feeding yourself the right fuels for the job. Everything else is about dealing with what's going on upstairs, in your head.

Alcohol is a means to an end. It's just a tool. And, given the right circumstances, that tool could be any other addiction.

Many people use TV as a coping strategy, getting all worked up about the fictional problems that a cheap soap opera character is going through. Others disappear from reality for a while by jumping into the world of video gaming or pornography. Some people use food to feel good about themselves, gorging themselves until they can't eat another bite. Or maybe the addiction is chasing money, seeing how many zeroes can be added to the bottom of a bank statement.

While none of these addictions might cause the physical harm that alcohol or other drugs can inflict, they're right up there when it comes to the psychological damage that can result.

Practice Makes Perfect

To become dependent on anything takes a lot of practice, it doesn't just happen overnight. If you practice something enough times, it will become a habit, and in certain circumstances the habit will form into an addiction. It's how our brain's works and it's how we get things done.

Imagine for a moment a life where you couldn't make any habits. Think about if you had to wake up every morning and relearn how to tie your shoe laces, or brush your teeth, or make the tea. Each of these tasks is a simple habit, a learned sequence of thoughts and actions that you've performed over and over, so much so that you can do them without even thinking.

The trick to building a habit is repetition. You repeat the same process time after time after time, until it becomes automatic.

Modeling Habits

Let's take an example.

When you first tried to tie your shoelaces, you didn't have a clue how to do it. You didn't know if the laces were arranged in your shoes correctly, you didn't know which part of the lace was supposed to go where, or the first thing about tying a proper knot.

You probably learned to tie your laces for the first time by modeling someone else, maybe your father or your older brother. They might have knelt next to you and asked you to watch them while they ran through the process in super slow motion. Maybe they taught you a little rhyme to help you to remember and practice the process.

After you'd done it a couple of times, with the help of your *"rabbit in the hole"* rhyme, you could probably fumble your way through a complete performance without any help. You still had to run each step through your mind before you could transfer the action to your fingers, but you had learned the basic technique.

Now, you've tied your shoelaces so many times that you could do it blindfolded, you don't have to think about it anymore.

A Life Full of Habits

If it wasn't for this ability to habitualize these simple processes in this way, we could never learn anything beyond the most rudimentary tasks. We wouldn't need to learn how to tie our shoe laces because there would be no such thing as shoes. If we couldn't habitualize our lives we'd still be stuck in the trees.

Everything we do is habitualized to one degree or another. Habits are what allow us to cross the road safely, or to read, to write, to speak, to play football, to dance a waltz, or the other million aspects of our lives that we so take for granted. Problems occur because our minds don't choose the things to habitualize based on what's good or bad, what's moral or immoral, or by what's logical or illogical.

Click Whirr - Repetition and Automaticity

So how does your mind know when it's time for the habit formation cycle to begin? The basic initiator and building block of any habit is repetition. Once you repeat an event more than a few times, you establish its importance. The event might be tying your shoelaces, looking left and right before you cross the road, or becoming addicted to a drug. The event doesn't matter, only the repetition. The more you repeat the same pattern, the more importance you're giving it. The higher the importance, the more building blocks are laid. The foundation becomes stronger, and it gets easier and easier for you to repeat over and over again.

Eventually you get to the stage where you're repeating the event without the need to think or even be aware that you're doing it. This is known as automaticity. Instead of having to think about doing something, you just do it. It becomes like a program running in the background. Something will happen to *trigger* the event and, with a click and a whirr, the program switches on automatically.

One of the secrets for fighting bad habits and creating new good habits is in breaking down and derailing these triggers. Each trigger is built around small details.

Sensual Selves

We interact with the outside world through our senses. Information comes in through these senses, is organized and interpreted in the brain, experienced through our emotions, compared with what we've experienced before, and either acted upon or ignored.

Even if you're just sitting in a chair, staring into space and not really thinking about much, there's a constant inflow of information coming in through your senses. The majority of this activity is perceived below the surface, so you're not consciously aware of it. But just because it's not hitting your conscious mind doesn't mean it's not being assimilated. Your subconscious registers almost everything to one degree or another.

Mind Filters

There's a variety of theories about the way incoming information is processed. One theory suggests that there are a series of filters set up between the electrical impulse arriving in your brain and getting through to your conscious awareness. The most important information gets through all the filters. Most of the information won't even get passed the first filter. Mostly, this data is all the background nonsense of the outside world, the noises and the smells and images that you don't need to process. This data is acknowledged only enough so it can be ignored.

Just like habits, these filters are an essential part of who we are. If there were no such filters, everything that came in through your senses would go straight into your conscious mind. You'd go doolally. Your mind would shut down like an overloaded electrical circuit.

Picture yourself walking down a busy main street and being aware of everything, every person who walked by you, every shout, every car horn, every movement, every smell, with nothing left out! Your mind registers all of these things, but you'll only be aware of 00.01%. Your awareness is confined to the things that might directly impact you. For instance, you'll notice the people who are in your path as you make your way along the sidewalk. You'll also notice any sudden or out of the ordinary sounds – like a car horn right beside you, or if someone shouts your name.

Awareness and perception are fascinating and very complex subjects and could fill up many volumes on their own. Suffice to say here that these internal filters are absolutely essential. They make it possible for you to live and thrive in this world.

Bar Smells

Once your habits are well established, many of the moment by moment details that comprise the habit lie between these filters and won't reach your awareness.

Let's look at an example, walking into your favorite bar. Think about everything that you experience from the time you walk into the bar until the time you leave. The sound of the door creaking as it opens, the sound of the other customers as you open the door, the smell of booze and crisps and people. Think about the familiar faces of the bar staff and the other regulars. Think about the familiar greetings as you walk towards your usual spot at the bar or your preferred table. The sounds of glasses clinking, beer taps pouring, cash registers opening and closing, the background music, the sports on the TV, and so on.

Each of these individual events generally happens in the background. You don't notice any of them; they're filtered before they get to your conscious mind. When something out of the ordinary happens, you suddenly become aware of the background. You hear a glass break, someone lets out a whoop because their team has scored a goal on the TV, the first sip of your pint tastes funny or it feels too warm, or you see a cockroach scurrying across the floor.

Reminders of the Familiar

When you stop drinking, however, all these ordinary background events become learned associations or triggers. The pop of a cork, the crack as the seal is broken on a new bottle of spirits, or the glugging as the liquid is poured into a glass. Because you're not taking part in the main action, you take in everything that's happening on the periphery. Everything that used to be in the background now acts as a sharp reminder of the thing that you're missing ... the alcohol.

Each learned association is woven into the familiar patterns that make up your drinking environment, be it your favorite bar or your favorite armchair at home. Each pattern adds another layer of complexity to your habit. So your habits end up being the sum of all these patterns, and like most things in life, the sum often exceeds the individual parts.

Overcoming the habit means breaking these triggers.

Breaking Triggers

One method of breaking a trigger is to change its meaning. You alter the perceptions, the thoughts, and the emotions that are attached to the triggers. When I used to drink, I always associated finishing work with having a nice cool pint of beer. In my mind, I was associating being thirsty with drinking beer. I broke this trigger by drinking water as soon as I finished work, or as soon as I was thirsty, so I never let myself get too thirsty. It didn't take very long to break the association and my thirst was better satisfied by the water than it ever was by drinking the beer.

A second way of breaking your triggers is to manipulate your environment. For instance, you can prevent a lot of triggers from firing off in your home by getting rid of the stuff that reminds you of drinking alcohol. Take all the booze out of the liquor cabinet and throw it away. Get rid of the glasses, the corkscrews, the beer mats, and so on.

Another way to break your triggers is to change your environment. You can stop the pub triggers by not going to the pub. You can stop other people from triggering your old habit by avoiding other drinkers for a while. And you drive home a different route that doesn't pass the liquor store/off-license.

Default Behaviors

By the time we get to adulthood, many of our fundamental defaults are already in place. For many of us, it's not a question of are we going to drink, only when. Most of us don't question the normalcy of drinking alcohol. We don't question the intelligence of putting a poison into our bodies indefinitely. We don't view alcohol as a drug or as a poison. All that conditioning has been laid well before we could legally buy our own booze.

Is this the fault of our parents? Yes and no! Yes, because it's up to our parents show us the way. They're our first teachers. It's their job to give us the right tools to face the world.

My son drinks and that's partly my fault. Our children learn by example. Tell a child not to drink and maybe he won't. If he sees most of the grown-ups using alcohol, he'll just assume that it's the normal thing to do and once he grows up, that's what he'll do as well.

But our parents were taught the same things by their parents. Our grandparents led by example just the same as our parents did. The same as I did!

Most of our western cultures are alcoholic. It's easy to be an alcohol user in an alcoholic culture. If the drug of choice was heroin, and that's not such a big leap as you might imagine, the majority of us may just be heroin users. Would we also be pretending that heroin wasn't a drug!

The reason many people have problems quitting drinking alcohol is because they're looking in the wrong place for the culprit. They're looking at the alcohol, when the real culprit is their own thinking and perceptions. Alcohol is only a means to an end. If you look at it from this angle, the solution is entirely in your control. You can look for guidance, but ultimately you are responsible for making the adjustments that will bring about your change.

Changing Automaticity!

"For imagination sets the goal picture which our automatic mechanism works on. We act, or fail to act, not because of will, as is so commonly believed, but because of imagination."
Maxwell Maltz

Cutting Your Hand Off for a Smoke

A friend of mine once described to me how quitting smoking was like having his right hand chopped off. After he'd lost his familiar crutch, he felt as if he had to relearn everything.

Smoking took up a large part of his life. The first thing he did when he woke up in the morning was smoke a cigarette. It was also the last thing he did before he got back into bed at night. He smoked before and after a meal, when he was on the phone, while he drove his car, on his lunch break, or any other time when he had a spare five minutes and wasn't restricted by the *anti-smoking police*. He smoked when he was happy, sad, or indifferent. He smoked as a distraction or to overcome his boredom. When he drank, he smoked twice as many cigarettes.

If you used to smoke, you'll probably get some of this. I can relate to it all. It took me over 100 attempts to quit smoking.

Relearning is Easy with a Gun to Your Head

Imagine if you had a freak accident and your right hand was chopped off, or your left hand if you're a southpaw. Everything that you take for granted suddenly becomes a struggle. Tying your shoelaces, writing, eating, cooking, catching, throwing, and playing are some of the things you'll need to relearn, not to mention clapping.

We all do these things without the need to think about them. But we were not born with the ability to do them, we had to learn as babies. Watch a new-born. They don't even realize that those little things floating in front of them are hands, let alone *their* hands. First they learn that these things are somehow in their control, and then they learn, bit by bit, how to control them.

This point was illustrated for me a few years ago by a friend who was born without any hands. He was a victim of the drug thalidomide, which had been sold in West Germany in 1957 to help pregnant mothers with morning sickness. Thousands of children were born with malformed limbs, a condition known as phocomelia; 60% of these children died. My friend was one of the survivors.

One day I told him that I had great respect because of what he'd achieved, despite his disability. He laughed, and in his broad German accent said "What fucking choice did I have!"

This was the way he was born; he didn't know he was missing hands until later in life. He never allowed his "disability" to prevent him from doing anything. Once he set his mind to doing something, he'd find a way. If something didn't work for him, he'd adapt to it or have it modified. For instance, his car was an automatic with a few minor adaptations to the steering wheel and the gear shift, which made them reachable.

Think > Adapt

It's a great attitude to life that most people could benefit from learning. Just because something seems impossible on the surface doesn't mean it's not possible. The answers to most of life's problems can be found with a little thinking and adaptation. Most people want the world to adapt to them instead of them adapting to the world.

What has all this got to do with changing habits? It doesn't matter if you lose your hands or you're quitting drinking, the same systems are in play. Whether you change through your own decision or because you've no choice in the matter, you'll use the exact same tools for adjusting your life to the new set of situations that you face.

The automaticity of any habit can be undone through our natural ability to think about change, to picture what life will be like when we change, and then to adapt and change. Awareness of the need to change is the first step. Breaking automaticity is about thinking and adjusting. Then it's about thinking some more and readjusting again. Rinse and repeat until you replace one automatic behavior with another.

You must also first go through your changes mentally before you can do them physically. So, you need to think about each step in your mind before you can put it into practice.

Moving Homes

"Repetition of the same thought or physical action develops into a habit which, repeated frequently enough, becomes an automatic reflex."
Norman Vincent Peale

Smooth Sailing

Moving house is an example of the effect of automaticity that most of us have experienced in our lives.

For instance, imagine that this is your normal routine before you move. You get out of the same side of the bed, maybe reach down and put on your slippers, and then you stand up and turn to the door on your right. You reach for the door handle, which is on the left side of the door, and pull the door toward you. You walk out of the bedroom, turn left into your bathroom, and use the loo, which is on your left as you go through the bathroom door. Once you finish with the loo, you turn around to the washbasin behind you, under the mirror. You wash your hands and take your toothbrush from the shelf above the sink. You put some toothpaste onto the bristles and brush your teeth. You might comb your hair or wash your face before finishing up and coming out of the bathroom and going into the kitchen to switch on the kettle or coffee maker.

You do all of this, and the hundreds of other moves that'll you'll make before you leave for work, using your habits, using your automaticity. You don't need to think about it. You'll only become aware of an action if something out of the ordinary happens; you pee on the floor or spill toothpaste all over yourself. Otherwise, you could almost do these things in your sleep.

Where's My Bloody Coffee????

This is what your life is like, thousands of routines spread throughout the day.

A big change is about to happen in your life, you are about to move home.

Moving home is one of the most stressful times in a person's life. One of the reasons for so much stress is because a lot of the automatic routines are non-transferable. You'll have to relearn everything.

You get through the move in one piece and you wake up in your home for the first morning. Perhaps your first thought is. *Where the hell am I?*

The bed is facing the wrong way. You haven't unpacked your slippers yet so they're not waiting for you as you swing your feet out onto the floor. You stand up and need to get your bearings. The door is in a completely different part of the room, so you have to think about which way to move. You walk to the door and automatically reach for the handle on the left side of the door. You're hand flaps about against the empty wood, trying to grasp the handle that's now on the right. Your bathroom is in the wrong place, as are your toilet and wash basin. Now you have to think about things every step of the way. All you want is coffee to wake you up, but where's the kitchen?

This feeling of confusion doesn't last long. You soon get used to the new layout. The unfamiliar quickly becomes the familiar.

Life's New Formation

It's the same process you'll go through when you quit drinking. A lot of things are going to be new, unfamiliar, and uncomfortable. You have lots of holes in your life that used to be filled by drinking. Don't worry, you're designed to adapt. You'll soon get used to the new layout of your life. The unfamiliar and the uncomfortable will soon become the familiar and the comfortable. You'll soon be adjusted, changed!

Chapter 6

Mindsets

"That's been one of my mantras - focus and simplicity. Simple can be harder than complex: You have to work hard to get your thinking clean to make it simple. But it's worth it in the end because once you get there, you can move mountains."
Steve Jobs

What is a Mindset?

A mindset is an attitude or mentality that you use when dealing with your life. Each mindset is a single or set of assumptions, a frame of mind, or a belief that you have developed through your experience and learning.

One simple example that we all know is the glass half empty or the glass half full mindset. The glass half empty frame of mind leans towards more pessimistic thinking. A glass half full mentality verges more towards the positive.

Fixed Vs Growth Mindsets

In her book, Mindset: The New Psychology of Success, Carol S. Dweck talks about two types of overall mindset, the fixed mindset and the growth mindset. The fixed mindset is based around the fundamental belief that you cannot change what you're born with. People with this mentality think that they are born with a fixed quota of intelligence, a fixed level of talent, and that throughout their lives, they have to take the hand they've been dealt with and do the best that they can within those limitations.

The growth mindset, on the other hand, is the belief that you are born with a starter pack of intelligence and talent. What you do with these attributes is up to you. People who have a growth mindset believe that they can cultivate their own successes, their own personalities, their own lives.

The growth mindset is all about believing that it is you who control the changes in your life, not the changes that control you. In the next couple of sections, we'll take a look at some of the change mindsets that you can cultivate to help you stop drinking for good.

Changing How You React to "Discomforts," i.e. Symptoms/Cravings/Side-Effects

"If you look for truth, you may find comfort in the end; if you look for comfort you will not get either comfort or truth only soft soap and wishful thinking to begin, and in the end, despair."
C. S. Lewis

Discomfort Mindset

The first mindset is that quitting drinking alcohol will cause you a little discomfort. That's it! For most people, there's nothing heavy or life threatening to contend with. The major battle is thinking the right thoughts. You can win this battle with little or no fuss if you put any ideas of death, of bad symptoms, of bad side effects, of bad cravings, and so on out of your mind.

If you're worried, go to your doctor and listen to what she has to tell you. Your aim is to be calm and logical about your quit before you start. Understand that it's not going to be easy, for all the reasons we've already gone through; but it is going to be simple.

We've already talked about the risk, so I'm not going to go into that again here. There are many people who will try to discourage you from the start by telling you that nobody should attempt to quit alcohol on her own. They don't know what they're talking about. There are millions of people who successfully have quit alcohol on their own.

The Discomfort Will Pass

The second mindset is that the discomfort is only short term, it will pass. Accept that you're going to feel uncomfortable for a while and just ride out that discomfort. Many of us can't remember back to when we didn't drink, so we've no reference point about how we should or shouldn't be feeling with no alcohol in our lives any more. There are many parts of our lives that have become deeply associated with alcohol and each of these associations can trigger the *alcohol itch*. You can't help that, it's all part of the habit. Over a short period of time, these triggers will lose their influence or they will become linked to something else. What you need to keep in mind is that if you don't feed the triggers, they will lose all their potency very fast.

Once you get past your first month, it gets a lot easier because you have some idea of what to expect. Alcohol will be out of your system, your life will be settling into new routines and new habits, and your sleep patterns should be stabilizing. Your thoughts about alcohol will become further and further apart. Week by week and month on month, you'll get used to being without drink; you'll build on this new database of what your life without alcohol looks like. From there on it will be a smooth ride.

You Hold the Discomfort Controls

The third mindset is that the level of discomfort you feel is very much in your control. If you dwell on how uncomfortable or how unfortunate you are, if you tell yourself that you can't stand it, or you can't do it any more, or you that don't want to feel like this, you're being your own worst enemy.

Instead, you can choose to think about how these discomforting feelings are going to recede and eventually fade away altogether. Concentrate and focus on how good your life is going to be once this happens.

Every minute is moving you one step closer to who you want to be and one step further away from your old life.

You can alter how you're thinking by physically doing something. Get up and move, go for a walk, do anything that takes your mind off drinking. If I found myself getting negative about what I was doing, I'd walk up and down the stairs in our apartment complex. That's about 200 steps from bottom to top. I'd climb up and down those stairs until I wasn't thinking about negativity any more. I couldn't do both things at once, being miserable about not drinking and being miserable about having to walk up and down these damned steps.

Comparing Your Discomfort

The fourth mindset is that the amount of discomfort you'll go through after you've quit is nothing in comparison to what you are going through right now and the pain that's waiting for you if you don't stop using this drug. Remember, the discomfort of quitting will pass with time; the discomfort of using alcohol only will get worse. You're at a crossroads in your life. Your choice involves pain, either way. You have to suck it up and take a few weeks of discomfort before moving onward into your new life, or you turn a blind eye toward your future. As always, the choice is yours!

The bottom line is you need to be comfortable feeling a bit of discomfort for a while - it's worth it.

Habit Memories

"A whole stack of memories never equal one little hope."
Charles M. Schulz

What is a Habit Memory?

A habit memory is a part of your old habit that has momentarily popped back into your awareness.

Although these habit memories can happen any time, they're usually triggered by something in your environment. They're set off by those associations that you previously linked with alcohol. As I said earlier, if you've been drinking for any number of years, you'll have a lot of these triggers.

Day to Day Triggers

Many of your triggers will be broken very quickly once you've quit. The first triggers to go are the associations that have been consistently linked with the day-to-day parts of your life. These routine triggers are things like finishing work and having a beer, having a drink with a meal or while you're watching TV, or having a few drinks over the weekend while you're out with your friends.

Once you quit drinking, you still need to carry on with your day to day life. You'll go to work in the morning and come home in the evening. You're still going to eat, you're still going to watch TV, and you're still going to socialize. When you constantly repeat these normal activities, day after day, the associations that they used to have with alcohol will weaken and eventually fail because they are no longer being reinforced.

Uncommon Triggers

Habit memories, on the other hand, are triggers that are associated with events in your life that don't happen every day. These are the once-a-year events like Christmas or Easter or your birthday. Or they occur infrequently like office parties, weddings, christenings, funerals, and so on.

Because these events only happen occasionally, they won't have gone through the consistent repetition that you used to deal with your routine triggers, so they might not have weakened enough to break. This is not a problem; the opposite can be said about these occasional triggers. They didn't have the same reinforcement as your routine triggers, so they won't be as strong in the first place.

The issue with these habit memories is that they can take you by surprise. The triggers that stand out at these occasions are the ones that are unique to the specific event. Toasts at the wedding for instance. Christmas is a time where there's going to be a lot of specific stimuli, stuff that won't be found at any other time. It might be just a set of triggers that haven't happened together since you quit. Let me give you an example.

Two plus Two Makes Five

About ten months after I quit, I got a phone call from a friend who's still living in Ireland. It's not unusual, I haven't seen him in since I came to Spain, but I've spoken to him several times over the phone.

It's always really great to catch up on what's going on back home. We tell each other stories about work, talk about the new Arsenal signings or how well the team is doing in the league, what different people are doing, just general nattering.

During this particular call, I asked him what he was up to. He said, *"I'm in Paddy Quinn's,"* which one of our old haunts, and *"I'm on my way to the Diamond in a minute"* - which was another one of our regular spots. In that moment, it felt to me like no time had gone by since I'd left Ireland. It was like I was just two miles up the road instead of two thousand miles away in a different country. I could taste the beer, smell the bar, see everything that was going on, and everyone who was in the bar. I almost said, *"I'll be down in a while!"*

The whole conversation had evoked a habit memory. It was a simple series of words that would have triggered my drinking in the past. Liam would call, I'd ask him where he was, he'd tell me which bar he was in, and I'd tell him - *"I'll be down in a while."* It was a very strong feeling that lasted only a couple of minutes. I didn't know what the hell was going on at first and it took me a while to understand just what had happened. Each of the elements of the conversation was nothing on its own. But tied together they made for a strong force.

Habit memories are a little overwhelming if you don't understand what's happening. It doesn't mean you're an alcoholic and it doesn't mean you're still thinking about drinking. It's just a mind trick. But it's good to be aware that this type of thought can sneak up on you.

Benefits of Quitting

"Failure is simply the opportunity to begin again, this time more intelligently."
Henry Ford

Hitting the Restart Button

What are the real benefits of quitting drinking? The real value, apart from getting rid of the toxins from your body, is that you have an open road ahead of you and so many different directions to choose from. It's a golden opportunity to re-think where you want your life to go.

In a way, making such a radical change in your life means that you get to hit the restart button. You get the chance to take a very close look at your life and that's not something that happens every day. Think about it. If you're on automatic pilot throughout your life, it can take something pretty heavy to break the spell. Because you're at the sticky end of an addiction, you get the c... look at your life with completely fresh eyes.

New Territories

This is not something that most "normal" people will ever do. How many people will ever look at their alcohol use as anything but "normal"? How many people will ever view alcohol as an impediment to their lives?

You are entering new territory where you'll learn how habits work. More importantly, you're going to learn how *your* habits work. That gives you massive edge in your life.

alcoholmastery.com, and AlcoholMasteryTV on YouTube, are all about guiding you through the basic principles of habit formation and habit breakdown, but only you have the ability to adapt those principles to yourself. You're the only one who can know what makes your habits unique. You're also in the best position to truly know where you want to go in your life, how you're going to get there, and to give yourself the best motivations to get the job done.

Real Time Adjustments

You will always perceive your habits playing out in real time. You get to observe each thought about each trigger as it happens, every sound, sight, feeling, taste, or smell. This means that you are in the best place to adjust in real time, eliminating or encouraging the triggers, depending on the direction you want each habit to take.

It's all part of the same process. You'll take similar steps to break a habit as you will to build a habit.

Believing Passionately

I am a great believer in the Law of Attraction. I'm not talking about the unusual belief that there's a force in the universe enabling you to make things appear in your life through some cosmic karmic influence. I don't know if that power exists, maybe it does, but I don't really care. That's completely out of my control.

A more realistic version of the Law of Attraction is that you are what you think you are. You control your thoughts and by controlling your thoughts you control your actions. What you think about yourself will always define who you are. What you think you can achieve in life is only ever as great as the limits you set for yourself. If you believe you can't do something, the chances are you won't do it. Belief is what makes everything possible.

Nikos Kazantzakis, author of *Zorba the Greek*, said, "*By believing passionately in that which does not yet exist, you create it. The non-existent is whatever we have not sufficiently desired.*"

Everything we ever do first requires a thought. The most fantastic and complex achievements of mankind, from landing a man on the Moon to saving the life of a premature baby, first had to be a single thought inside the mind of a single human being.

You need to understand that this addiction is not about the alcohol. It's not about this evil thing that's hell-bent on taking control of your life. It's all about you. It's about your thoughts, your perceptions, your habits, and how you interpret your background and your culture. Looking at your life from this perspective gives you the ability to change anything.

Living Your Life like A Scientist

"All life is an experiment. The more experiments you make the better."
Ralph Waldo Emerson

What Happens If...?

We're all born as scientists. We explore, we test, we adjust and test some more. We want to see what happens if...! What happens if I put my finger in there? What happens if I jump into that puddle? What does this taste like? Will it taste different if I put it into my mouth the other way around? What happens if I put one foot in front of the other? What happens if I do it faster?

When we're young, we're excited to perform a seemingly never ending stream of experiments. Unfortunately, this type of behavior is only tolerated up until a certain age. Then we're forced to sit still, not to ask silly questions, and to just accept that which we are told.

It's time for you rediscover your inner scientist again, to ask what happens if ...?

Try, Fail, Learn, Adjust...

Nothing works for everyone except experimentation. As long as you're always willing to experiment, to try and fail, you'll always figure out what works.

The sequence is simple. Try, fail, learn, adjust; try, fail, learn, adjust; try, fail, learn, adjust; ... try – succeed!

You keep trying until you find the success! After each fail, you go over the things that went right and those that went wrong. Then you run the whole process through again, taking into account what you've just learned in the previous iteration. Rinse and repeat! Rinse and repeat! You cannot fail to achieve your success once you keep trying.

Every transformation starts out as a single adjustment. Adjustments are the building blocks for constructing whatever you want to have or to achieve in life. They're the foundation of your success blueprint.

Life Without Alcohol

While you're drinking alcohol, most great things are simply impossible because of the wasting nature of the habit. While you're sleeping off the alcohol, you can't do the things you need to do to achieve your dreams. While you're spending your time hungover, you can't spend it being productive. While your brain is steeped in alcohol, how can it think the great thoughts that create the great values in your life!

I used to fear what my life would look like without alcohol. I feared that my life would be empty and hollow. *How will I socialize? Will I lose all my friends? Will I be a miserable bastard forever?*

Now, I fear ever drinking again!

Note from the Author

Thank you so much for supporting Alcohol Mastery by reading *Stop Drinking Alcohol*. What can you do next?

Audiobook Version

If you would like to purchase the audio version of this eBook, you can get it on the Alcohol Mastery website: http://alcoholmastery.com/stop-drinking-alcohol/

Reviews

If *Stop Drinking Alcohol* was helpful to you, I would really appreciate you leaving an honest review on amazon.com. Amazon pays attention when readers show enthusiasm for a book, so ratings and reviews make a big difference in getting the word out. If you've already left a review, a big THANK YOU!

Hundreds of Free Videos

Come take a look at the website at: http://alcoholmastery.com where you'll find plenty of posts, videos, and audio about my whole simple to quit alcohol philosophy.

You'll also find weekly videos (almost weekly) about my adventure so far. The videos start from the very first day I quit drinking. I still cringe when look back on that first video. It was the first time I'd ever made a video for YouTube, so my presentation skills were very raw, quickly learned from a *Dummies* book if I remember rightly.

When I look at that person on the screen, on the one hand I feel very sorry for who I was - the product of over 30 years living under the illusion that drinking alcohol was normal. But on the other hand, I feel elated about the journey which is about to unfold for that man. It's very satisfying to look back with a sense of detachment at the man I was and to understand how far along my personal road I've traveled, just by getting alcohol out of the equation.

It's an eye opening experience that I would recommend to anyone. Use whatever you've got, a video camera, phone, or go and buy a cheap camera. Sit down and spend some time recording yourself talking about who you are in that moment and what you want to get out of life now that you've made the decision to quit. Record a message for your future self about how you feel now and where you want to go, about the person you want to become... it's very, very powerful. You don't have to show it to anyone else, you can keep it locked up forever. When you need to look back, you'll have an emotional reminder of how far you've come. That person, who's talking to you on the screen from your past, can give you some very compelling reasons to stay motivated and focused on what you need to do to succeed.

Apart from my personal journey, you'll find a lot of videos offering tips and tricks about the stuff I've learned that you could benefit from, as well as questions and answer sessions, and some general rambling. It's all there for you to browse through for free, 24/7. Hopefully you'll find some inspiration in there somewhere.

You can get the free Alcohol Mastery Podcast on iTunes by clicking here or on the website by clicking on the podcast link in the menu at the top of the page.

To be sure you get notifications of everything, you can sign up to the Alcohol Mastery Newsletter here. You'll get news of any new video or podcast episode, along with scoops on all the new projects.

If you're a fan of social media, you can find Alcohol Mastery by clicking on these links: Facebook and Twitter

Feel free to contact me at any time through the contact form on the website, by direct message through the Facebook page, or you can email me here: kevin@alcoholmastery.com.

All the best to you!

Kev

Onwards and Upwards!

CPSIA information can be obtained
at www.ICGtesting.com
Printed in the USA
LVHW111447261118
598286LV00001B/255/P